TREK CELEBRATION TWO

EDITED BY JAMES VAN HISE

PIONEER BOOKS, INC
LAS VEGAS, NV

(800)444-2524 Ext 67

PIONEER BOOKS

MTV: MUSIC YOU CAN SEE   ISBN#1-55698-355-7
TREK: THE NEXT GENERATION CREW BOOK   ISBN#1-55698-363-8
TREK: THE PRINTED ADVENTURES ISBN#1-55698-365-5
THE CLASSIC TREK CREW BOOK   ISBN#1-55698-368-9
TREK VS THE NEXT GENERATION   ISBN#1-55698-370-0
TREK: THE NEXT GENERATION TRIBUTE BOOK ISBN#1-55698-366-2
THE HOLLYWOOD CELEBRITY DEATH BOOK   ISBN#1-55698-369-7
LET'S TALK: AMERICA'S FAVORITE TV TALK SHOW HOSTS   ISBN#1-55698-364-6
HOT-BLOODED DINOSAUR MOVIES ISBN#1-55698-365-4
BONANZA: THE UNOFFICIAL STORY OF THE PONDEROSA   ISBN#1-55698-359-X

EXCITING NEW TITLES SOON TO BE RELEASED

THE KUNG FU BOOK   ISBN#1-55698-328-X
TREK: THE DEEP SPACE CELEBRATION   ISBN#1-55698 330-1
MAVERICKS: TV'S WESTERN HEROES   ISBN#1-55698-334-4
TREK: THE DEEP SPACE CREW BOOK   ISBN#1-55698-335-2
MARRIAGE & DIVORCE -HOLLYWOOD STYLE   ISBN#1-55698-333-6
THE LITTLE HOUSE COMPANION   ISBN#1-55698-332-8
TREK: THE NEXT GENERATION TRIBUTE BOOK TWO ISBN#1-55698-329-8
TREK: THE ENCYCLOPEDIA   ISBN#1-55698-331-X

COVER BY MORRIS SCOTT DOLLENS

Library of Congress Cataloging-in-Publication Data
James Van Hise, 1949—

Trek Celebration 2

1. Trek Celebration 2 (television, popular culture)
I. Title

First Printing, 1994

Publisher and Designer: Hal Schuster   *Editor: David Lessnick*

CONTENTS

DEDICATED
TO
DREAMERS

TREK CELEBRATION TWO

Part One—
ABOARD
THE ENTERPRISE

MANN's CHINESE THEATRE, December 5, 1991, as the
STAR TREK cast poses for an unused cover shot for ENTER-
TAINMENT WEEKLY.

Photo by Chris Flicker

"You don't watch that, do you?"

I wish I had a dollar for every time somebody asked me that question upon noticing my key chain, which bears a somewhat out-of-character smiling Spock and the glib slogan, SPOCK FOR PRESIDENT.

Yes, I watch STAR TREK and have for almost as long as it's been around. I don't really know whether Spock, if he existed, would make a good president or not; I haven't really considered it. You see, despite what a lot of newspaper reporters say, STAR TREK fans are not poor, misguided souls who are more at home with the myriad of fictional characters parading through their minds in dubiously short skirts and a '60s velour, than with the real world.

It was his wish to write truthfully about the real world which prompted Gene Roddenberry to create STAR TREK in the first place. There was plenty to write about in his younger days, subjects about which many writers longed to be permitted to speak frankly. But those were the sixties. Hampered by censorship and the post-war narrow-mindedness that so many of his peers were obliged to put up with, Roddenberry came to the conclusion that he should either give up his writing career altogether or find another way to put his message across. Luckily he chose the latter. Thus STAR TREK was born, and with it a forum for many talented writers bursting with ideas, making statements which would not have been allowed on the airwaves in any other form than as science fiction.

BY VALERIE HERD

Sadly, despite the welcoming fanfare of its young public, brilliant casting choices and intuitive story ideas, STAR TREK was doomed not long after its introduction to the US populace, or was it? like some martyred public figures of that era, STAR TREK lives on, in poster form, on video, in syndication, molded in plastic, etched in gold. . . and melded into the hearts of many who will doubtless pass on the word of "IDIC" as long as they can draw breath.

Almost thirty years on, fans continue to tend the STAR TREK flame. James T. Kirk's trekdom is now widely known as "Classic STAR TREK," the eternally youthful-on-TV crew is joined by members of two spin-offs, both set in Gene Roddenberry's fictional universe where humanity has learned tolerance and acceptance, having all but erased the scars of past times' racism, bigotry and injustice.

The Enterprise-D, captained by a Frenchman named Picard, is larger than the original Enterprise; perhaps a product of a richer Federation which has successfully added the membership of many more strange new worlds since Kirk's time. Picard and his crew have been born in an even more tolerant epoch where, it seems, the display of most human emotions is frowned upon (too much involvement with Vulcans?).

The new Enterprise crew now travels farther, talks longer, and involves themselves more in the technological aspects of their off-worldly lives and have encountered an incredibly long list of English-speaking alien races sporting a variety of scales, bumps and headgear. Gone are the nymphs in filmy gowns, women with well-developed thighs and impossible hair arrangements, and men with a watch-it-mister attitude.

But despite the more staid, sophisticated behavior of the new age Federation characters, STAR TREK in its new forms still carries with it Roddenberry's message that if humanity could only overcome its own failings, great things might be achieved! STAR TREK, born in the post-Camelot era in which many people aspired to 'find themselves,' has grown up, and its original viewers with it.

The message carried by the original STAR TREK episodes still rings true today, and they have been joined by new tales of terrorism, racism, discrimination and torture, courtesy of the real world, as seen by the writing staff of STAR TREK—THE NEXT GENERATION and its sister spin-off. Subjects which all too often cause viewers to reach for the channel changer hold them in rapt attention when broached by the gallant captains of either of the two ships named Enterprise, or by the politically-correct, coolly intelligent

THE ROSE PARADE float of NEXT GENERATION'S Enterprise on January 2, 1991.

Photo by Chris Flicker

commander of that huge steering-wheel-in-the-sky, Deep Space Nine.

Perhaps humankind is not yet ready for involvement with extraterrestrial intelligence, or to journey peacefully amongst the stars, but Gene Roddenberry's legacy lives on to act as a guide for some, a bright flame of hope for others, and continues to broadcast the promise that humanity may, after all, live long and prosper.

The STAR TREK universe. Today it seems never-ending, but where and how did it begin and what is at the core of it?

STAR TREK: Once a long shot, now a legend. And what becomes a legend most? More than a quarter of a century of unending fan adulation, syndicated reruns, major motion pictures and successful spin-offs. But none of these things would exist if they could not stand upon the firm foundation of that legend: the original, classic STAR TREK. What, exactly, made a legend of Gene Roddenberry's "Wagon Train In Space"? Let's take a brief look.

The essence of STAR TREK is composed of some basic but potent elements. These are the building blocks that have made such enduring icons of Kirk, Spock, McCoy and their crew. First, the camaraderie between the members of that crew, often tested by their differing philosophies but, ultimately, unbreak-

able. Add to this the basic idea that all living, thinking beings are created equal, the essential notion that universal harmony is not only desirable, but possible. This open minded viewpoint is the very heart of STAR TREK. And the third element? Action! Never was there such a two-fisted champion of peaceful interstellar relations as Jim Kirk, and STAR TREK, like most of the TV shows of the '60s, had more than its share of knock-down, drag-out slugfests, highlighted by William Shatner's own unique brand of fisticuffs.

When Gene Roddenberry created STAR TREK in 1966, he fully expected the series to last at least five years. But he never imagined that STAR TREK would be alive and flourishing 30 years later. Even to

Roddenberry the futurist, such an idea would have seemed unlikely.

THE 23rd CENTURY IN 1964

It was a turbulent time when Roddenberry conceived STAR TREK, shortly after the assassination of President Kennedy. The civil rights movement was active, and strife in the U.S.A. was a commonplace event. Roddenberry reacted to this by conceiving a future in which humanity had survived its struggles and conquered the stars. STAR TREK was optimistic when few people were optimistic about anything, defiantly proclaiming that we would survive these difficult days.

Science fiction on television was not common during this period; to sell the concept to a skeptical network, Roddenberry cloaked it in familiar terms, describing it as "WAGON TRAIN to the stars." The network bought his pitch. Once Roddenberry had made the pilot episode of STAR TREK, "The Cage," NBC took a look at it. They found it interesting, but "too cerebral." And yet they liked it enough to offer to pay for a second pilot— so long as Roddenberry got rid of the female character, Number One, and the Satanic alien named Spock.

SPOCK: THE ALIEN WITHIN US

What would STAR TREK have been like without Spock? The character was an important part of the ensemble, adding vital elements to certain stories. Would STAR TREK have achieved its longevity if Kirk and McCoy had been the big two on the series? We'll never know, for NBC let Spock stay, and Roddenberry grafted certain aspects of the discarded Number One onto the Vulcan to create a new take on the character. The Spock of "Where No Man Has Gone Before" was a different alien than the Spock of "The Cage." Within four episodes, Spock's inner turmoil came boiling to the surface in "The Naked Time," revealing his unspoken love for his mother and his shame at feeling friendship for Kirk. Spock the outsider and outcast was born, and the viewers never forgot this baring of his soul. His cold, cool exterior was a mask. He wasn't such an alien figure after all. He was as torn up inside about how he fit into the world around him as many of those who watched that show. It was inevitable that a vast following would build up around the character overnight.

Essentially, Spock appeals to the viewer because he embodies a basic human dilemma. Everyone would like to maintain complete control over their emotions, running their lives with cool logic and never suffering the emotional turmoil that is our given lot as humans. Spock seems to represent that idea: the ultimate in cool. But there is a price to pay, as seen on those few occasions when Spock's control was shaken. It is these moments that reinforce Spock's appeal, because they prove that, underneath all that collected and calm facade, he's really just like the rest of us! A truly emotionless entity would either be uninvolving or completely frightening; Spock's inner core of humanity transcends all that, making him a true cultural icon.

THE NEW MAN IN CHARGE

In "The Cage," we see a commander of the Enterprise who is much different from James T. Kirk. Captain Pike, played by Jeffrey Hunter, finds the responsibilities of command a heavy burden to bear. He is seriously considering resigning his commission and leaving Starfleet. What bothers him is that any decision he makes on an almost daily basis could result in the death of one of his crew, and he recently saw just that happen. Pike just didn't want to be responsible for any more lives, or deaths.

On the other hand, in the second pilot, "Where No Man Has Gone Before," William Shatner portrayed Captain Kirk as a commander who took his command no less seriously than Pike, but who did not let it weigh on him. He faced the hard choices and he made them, even when it involved Gary Mitchell, one of his oldest friends.

The appeal of Kirk is that he is (in the original series) a youthful, vigorous man, a true explorer who is keen only on discovery, not on conquest. He possesses a basic joy of life that drives his every move, whether it be entering a new and fascinatingly strange area of space, or a new and fascinatingly beautiful woman. In many ways, he's just a regular guy, obsessed with his car and happy to drive around all over the place with his friends. However, his car is no Chevy, but a massive star ship, and one of his friends has pointed ears and copper-based blood! Canny, resourceful, and single-minded when it becomes necessary, James Kirk seems to be good at everything, and does it all with a real flair that lifts him above mere competence into the realm of brilliance.

Kirk is the hero we all aspire to be. And while many have dispar-

Nichelle Nichols at MANN's CHINESE THEATRE on
December 5, 1991.

Leonard Nimoy at MANN's CHINESE THEATRE on December 5, 1991.

Photo by Chris Flicker

aged Shatner's acting, there can be no denying that his is Kirk. Just try to imagine a STAR TREK in which one of the actors considered before Shatner had been chosen. Lloyd Bridges would have been good, probably, but totally different. Try to imagine STAR TREK with Jack Lord as Kirk! We're all fortunate that things turned out the way that they did.

THE BIG THREE

When STAR TREK was picked up as a series, DeForest Kelley became the new ship's doctor, Leonard "Bones" McCoy, a role that filled out the final ingredient in the chemistry that made STAR TREK great. Almost a cynic, but motivated by his overwhelming passion for life and the living, McCoy is the voice within us all that cries out at what is wrong in the world about us, seeking solutions while fighting the distressing suspicion that there is nothing to be done.

McCoy's addition to the cast created a three-part chemistry between Kirk, Spock and McCoy, something which is difficult to achieve in an ongoing series. This chemistry contributed much to the reasons why the series still holds up under repeated viewings. Even when we know exactly what's going to happen scene after scene, watching the interaction among the three stars makes for highly entertaining viewing. The three personalities are very different and yet they managed to compliment one another in the way they work together.

When you have three characters who clearly function as well together as these three, it opens up many possibilities for the writers to explore, which they did whenever possible. Kirk is the decisive commander. Spock's cool logic points out the unpleasant necessities while McCoy challenges these decisions based on their human cost. And yet these three are friends. They are just three very different people. It wasn't long before entire episodes were spun around stories involving just these three characters. This is particularly true of "The City On The Edge Of Forever," "Mirror, Mirror," "Mantrap" and "Miri," just to name a few.

PEACEFUL WARRIORS

Now that we've considered these characters, it is important to consider , precisely what they were doing out there in outer space. Theirs was a peaceful mission of contact and exploration. Although they were heavily armed, their possible excesses were held in check by the Prime Directive. Under this all-important Federation rule, all cultures and entities were held to be worthy of equal respect and consideration. While many right-wingers today would dismiss this as "cultural relativism" or some such other dismissive term, the fact of the matter is that STAR TREK's appeal is basically to the liberal sentiment.

This philosophy was really what caught the hearts and minds of the generation that first viewed this program with such wonder back in the '60s. While the world around them was burning with the never-ending struggle to establish such a humane world, both at home and abroad, here was a TV show which depicted a future in which our world had achieved such a fine balance, and was ready to share it with the universe! STAR TREK's basic philosophy fits right in with the dawning of the Age of Aquarius, an age still yearning to be born. Who knows? Perhaps STAR TREK will turn out to be one of the keys to our brighter future. That hope is certainly the heart and soul of STAR TREK's undying appeal.

FIGHTIN' FOR PEACE

On the other hand, it does seem that STAR TREK's heroes, particularly Kirk, frequently expressed their noble ideas with a sharp right hook, phaser blast or Vulcan neck pinch. Part of this simply derives from the time during which the original STAR TREK was created. In the '60s, shows which weren't outright dramas were quickly categorized and expected to deliver a certain type of story. Science fiction shows, as well as westerns and cop shows, were expected to deliver more than just cerebral adventures. This is why STAR TREK seems to have a certain quotient of fist-fights. These are particularly evident in "This Side of Paradise," "Space Seed," "Shore Leave" and "Mirror, Mirror." Ironically, this sort of violence— also seen to good effect on other shows like THE WILD, WILD WEST— was the focus of some outraged citizens who decried violence on television and its evil influence on children. Today, with shows like COPS on every day, the violence in STAR TREK seems almost quaint by comparison. There was an innocence to it. It wasn't about Kirk and his team hurting anybody, but about the need to defend themselves in the rough-and-tumble frontier worlds of space. Kirk could take on any villain himself, a basic requirement for any hero. It's all very well and good to spread peace and harmony throughout the universe, but there's no need to be a wimp about it. What saves STAR TREK from becoming a wishy-washy sermon was the fact that Kirk and crew could take care of themselves.

Part of STAR TREK's eternal appeal rests on the fact that all its messages and olive branches were part of well crafted adventure stories that kept the eye as well as the mind engaged.

A SHOW WITH SOMETHING TO SAY

STAR TREK has always possessed a degree of social commentary, whether it be obvious such as in "Let That Be Your Last Battlefield," or subdued such as in "A Taste of Armageddon" in which a planetary government attempted to fight a clean war which didn't disrupt its society with overt battles and destructive conflicts. But the approach to its social commentary was always done carefully.

STAR TREK in the '60s still managed to inspire people with what it had to say and what it showed us. By suggesting that such a glittering future was not only probable but possible, it inspired people to want to be a part of that future. There are scientists today working for NASA, the military and elsewhere who were inspired as chil-

dren to see the exciting possibilities in science and the ways it could affect the future. STAR TREK is still infecting people with that excitement today. Its noble ideas, fast-paced adventure and close-knit team of regular characters are elements that have withstood the test of time.

With STAR TREK—THE NEXT GENERATION, Gene Roddenberry transplanted his humanistic ideals whole, showing how the 24th century had produced an even more liberal and open-minded mankind than the 23rd century had. These ideals of Gene's suffused STAR TREK and they live on in the series years after Roddenberry's passing.

STAR TREK—THE NEXT GENERATION has entered its seventh season in spite of doubters who didn't believe it would ever see a third. What has enabled it to survive and how has it adapted to the very different world and audience expectations of today?

STAR TREK—THE NEXT GENERATION is that rarest of things, a spin-off that not only came into existence nearly twenty years after its predecessor, but which also managed to surpass it in first-run longevity. THE NEXT GENERATION has

Chapter Two
A LOOK AT THE NEXT GENERATION

tial character over the course of six years, often contradicting notions held sacred in the earlier STAR TREK canon. While some early episodes, like "The Naked Now" (the obvious choice) tried to hard to point up the links with the original TREK,

taken off in its own course, but it does share some basic qualities with the original classic STAR TREK. In fact, at its best, it takes STAR TREK's basic philosophies even farther than they were able to go in the original series. Religion, women, sex and other cultures all get a better deal, all in all, today than they did in Roddenberry's '60s.

NEW GENERATION, NEW VIEWS

But even so, THE NEXT GENERATION has created its own essen-

others tried equally hard to be different, most notably "Skin Of Evil," which erroneously tried to show a hard, modern edge by heavy-handedly killing off a regular character. In time, the true essence of THE NEXT GENERATION came into light.

For instance, the cultural open-mindedness in THE NEXT GENERATION does not reflexively discard religion or spiritual matters as mindless drivel. "Who Watches The Watchers" veered awfully close to that old science fiction view of religion as an evil needing to be eradicated (a post-Marxist position if ever there was one), but Klingon culture, more fully examined in THE NEXT GENERATION, clearly has a vital and central religious element, and Worf seems to be the first Enterprise crew member to actually have a religion! There were even touches of mysticism in the superb episode "The Inner Light."

True, old-style elements emerge even here: the Klingon messiah Kehless, for example, turns out to be a clone of the original ancient hero in "Rightful Heir." But the Klingon religion is not thrown out the window because of this. Even though certain Klingon priests are revealed as manipulators, Worf's mystical leanings still remain of central importance to him, and no one on THE NEXT GENERATION would ever try to convince him to give it up and become a secular humanist!

NO MORE MINISKIRTS

Women have a better place in THE NEXT GENERATION than they did in '60s STAR TREK. Two are in regular positions of authority, while a third occupies an intriguing position as the future's greatest bartender. This is a far cry from the days of Kirk, when all women in space except Uhura (who only got to say "hailing frequencies open, sir" most of the time) seemed to have just come from their night jobs as go-go dancers, and were dressed accordingly.

Neither Doctor Beverly Crusher nor Counsellor Deanna Troi can be marginalized the way Uhura so often was (although it should be noted how important it was just for Uhura to be there answering the phone, as it were, a fact often attested to by Whoopi Goldberg). And their presence, along with that of Dr. Catherine Pulaski during the second season, signals that this is a show about a future where the sexes have really achieved equality. Women characters abound everywhere in the background, in every job on the Enterprise, and no one would ever dare to treat them as sex objects. (Although THE NEXT GENERATION has occasionally used Deanna Troi for a bit of sex appeal, gratuitous cleavage and all. . .)

FUTURE SEX

This is not to say that there is no sex in the Twenty-Fourth Century. In fact, there seems to be even more than there was in the Twenty-Third, which is pretty amazing when you consider just how much Jim Kirk got around in his day. Every major character has been involved in at least one romantic entanglement that faded knowingly to black just as a commercial interruption cut in at the very nick of time.

No one really knows what Barclay really got up to on the holodeck before his problem was revealed. Even Data got lucky once, and Wesley Crusher had a crush on an alien girl one time, although that apparently remained platonic. Off the top of my head, it seems uncertain just which NEXT GENERATION character has been most active in this arena, but odds are that it was either Deanna Troi or Will Riker, who themselves were once involved with each other before the series proper began. And their attitude of friendship, after their previous affair, also points at a greater sophistication than was ever shown in STAR TREK; Jim Kirk always had serious trouble with his ex-girlfriends! And THE NEXT GENERATION has veered into some peculiar sexual situations from time to time: Beverly Crusher having sex with an alien who was borrowing Will Riker's body in "The Host" being the most obvious example, as well as Riker's involvement with an androgynous character in "The Outcast."

SOCIAL ISSUES REDUX

These two episodes stand as examples of one of THE NEXT GENERATION's weak points: its handling of social issues. While this may in fact be no more heavy-handed than it was on the original STAR TREK, it seems more out of place here. While THE NEXT GENERATION has presented many thoughtful stories that dealt with modern questions in one form or another, it seems to come up a cropper whenever it tries the head-on, or "Yang-vs-Com" approach.

In "The Host," Beverly Crusher was open-minded enough to sleep with her parasitic Trill lover while it was occupying Riker's body, but balked when it turned up in a female host body. The attempt, in "The Outcast," to somehow turn around the problems faced by gays in our society and make it understandable to the "regular guy," fell flat on its face when it made it seem as if Riker was going up against a planet of man-hating lesbians! Another, earlier episode really botched a story on drug addiction in an equally inept fashion. And this is all the more bothersome when you consider the generally high quality of the writing on STAR

TREK—THE NEXT GENERATION.

WORDS, NOT DEEDS

And this leads to one of the greatest strengths of the series: it is an hour long drama, not a weekly action/adventure program. True, elements of action often enter into the stories of THE NEXT GENERATION, but the basic format centers on the telling of well-wrought tales with a science-fiction theme. The failure of certain episodes to create believable drama while tackling an issue-of-the-week pales beside the many fine dramas that have touched on deeper human issues in the course of their unfolding.

A simple "bottle show" like "The Drumhead" became an insightful study of the miscarriage of justice when an inquiry into an onboard explosion snowballs into one woman's obsessive quest to uncover a threat which does not exist. The ongoing saga of Worf presented an ever-deepening view of the mysterious culture of the Klingons. THE NEXT GENERATION has taken chances and violated its own premises to good effect: "First Contact" broke from format radically to present an excellent tale of pre-contact maneuverings gone wrong, while "Hollow Pursuits" introduced a character (played by Dwight Schultz) who had more than a few things wrong with him. THE NEXT GENERATION has, in general, a much more sophisticated take on life than the classic STAR TREK did in its day. Even when it breaks format again and has an action oriented episode like "Starship Mine," the effect is new and stimulating, if only by comparison with the norm.

POST-GENE PC

Another crucial element of THE NEXT GENERATION is that it is far more politically correct than the original STAR TREK. Its more enlightened treatment of women is a prime example of this. It's good to see THE NEXT GENERATION's view of a future in which Rush Limbaugh would probably be permanently unfomfortable. And although Roddenberry's dictum that there would be no conflict between crew members has limited interpersonal dramas somewhat, it has prevented the show from becoming an outer-space soap opera.

It does re-create, in its own fashion, one of the elements that gave the original STAR TREK its greatest strength: a central cast of characters that obviously functions like an extended family of sorts. Who could ask for anything more in real life, anyway: a great and exciting job for a company with obviously great benefits, working with your friends instead of strangers.

STAR TREK—THE NEXT GENERATION succeeds primarily by realizing the basic strengths of the original STAR TREK all over again, refined to a greater polish and a deeper lustre, avoiding the pitfalls that occasionally tripped up the original, and generally avoiding new pitfalls of its own. Its cast and characters, its stories and its smooth style, all appeal to the younger audience of the '90s while keeping most of the old-time faithful happy as well. There can be no doubt that THE NEXT GENERATION keeps the flame of Gene Roddenberry's prophetic vision alive and well today, and will carry on well into the next century!

When STAR TREK—THE NEXT GENERATION completed its first season, fans were ready for an honest, no-holds-barred review of the show. The following includes some of those comments from the first couple seasons of TNG, as well as some on its most recent season.

When STAR TREK—THE NEXT GENERATION premiered in 1987 it was greeted with both praise and derision, as the following different reactions from a variety of fan points of view attest to.

ACCORDING TO JEFFERSON SWYCAFFER

Chapter Three

THE NEXT GENERATION: A CRITICAL REPORT

I like ST—TNG better than old original STAR TREK. Old Trek played a cute game an awful lot: get the boys into trouble, a problem that they just couldn't solve. . . and then have the Enterprise rise over the hill like the cavalry riding to the rescue. Cute, emotionally satisfying, but intellectually vacant. (This was used to its fullest possible effect in the fifth movie. A lovely scene. . . but is it meaningful? No. It's cartooney.)

COMPARABLE HIGH POINTS

Old Trek had some marvelous shows. No doubt about it. "Requiem for Methuselah," "City on the Edge of Forever," "Devil in the Dark."

New Trek has had some beauties also: "Measure of a Man"—the trial where Data must prove his legal right to sentience and liberty. "Elementary Dear Data"—the discovery of Professor Moriarty on the holodeck. "Sarek"—the first TNG appearance of Sarek and his emotional loss of control. Or "First Contact"—where Riker is captured by a planet that has a '20th century' level of technological advancement.

Sure, TNG has had clunkers; some really cruddy shows. Some barfulous three-baggers and ankle-walking toads that ought to be spun down in a blender and used to fill freeway potholes.

New Trek succeeds better in fixing a tone. Remember the episode with the strange "time hiccups"? The music, the pacing, the special effects, all worked together to lend this a spooky, eerie tone which was astonishingly sophisticated and effective.

Or "Yesterday's Enterprise" where the uniforms, the lighting and even the emotional tone of the acting all built up into a sense of alienness, showing what the Enterprise would be like as a true warship. Compare this episode to the "Mirror, Mirror" episode of Old Trek where the only difference was in the abandoned vulgar sensuality of the acting, but otherwise only trivial differences were utilized to set the tone. The advances in filmmaking arts and sciences show a steady improvement over the decades.

NEXT GENERATION cast members at THE AMERICAN TELEVISION AWARDS.

Photo © 1993 Albert L. Ortega

THE DEBATE

No question in STAR TREK circles has provoked as much debate as the question of which show is better. Old original STAR TREK or STAR TREK—THE NEXT GENERATION. I think it is important to view each show in its own historical context. Only this way can the individual character of each show be seen clearly, and false points of comparison can be avoided.

Remember that Jean-Luc Picard, the Captain of the Enterprise in TNG, is very much a '60s character, while Captain Kirk is a character who could only exist in the late '80s.

How's that again? Did you just blink and miss something?

Well, certainly: Picard is a pacifist, a gentle person who governs by consensus, a man to whom war is an abomination. It seems perfectly clear that he was created by writers working during the peace-loving '60s.

Kirk, on the other hand, is clearly a product of the bellicose '80s, the era of Rambo, the Reagan-Bush era of small, overwhelming victories. Kirk benefits from all the vigor of the post-feminists, post-stagnation, post-peace decade.

KIRK AND PICARD

Picard attempts to talk with his enemies, just as the U.S. attempted to talk with the leadership of the North Vietnamese government at the famous Paris Peace Talks. Picard is very well suited to diplomatic dialogue. Patrick Stewart is gifted with a deep, smooth, eloquent voice and he delivers the sweet speech of reason in a very persuasive manner.

Kirk, on the other hand, has thirty years of hindsight which Picard lacks, and knows that peace negotiations are generally fruitless. Kirk opens fire; Kirk lets fly; Kirk sees through his enemies' tricks and blasts them from the sky. The parallels to the operations against Grenada, Panama, Libya and Iraq are unmistakable.

The other parallels simply fill in this point. In New Trek, Picard's ship has civilians and families aboard, in a very homey, wholesome, "family oriented" program, which obviously reflect the Headstart and VISTA Peace Corps mentality of the time. But in Old Trek, Kirk runs a modern war machine, a professional, goal-oriented ship far more relevant to today's military service.

Picard is in constant contact with the politicians back home, which is a sad historical reminder of how over-centralized the Federal government was in the '60s. But Kirk is free to operate as he sees fit, a reflection of the Norman

Schwartzkopf approach to military solutions.

THE DIFFERENCES IN THE CREW

The supporting cast also points out the essential differences between the '60s and the '80s.

Data, the personable android, hints at the idea, fashionable in the '60s, that computers could solve any problem, even problems not suitable for computation. By the time of New Trek, of course, people had come to understand that computers are fine for some tasks but completely wrong for others. Kirk is constantly blowing up computers which had gone insane from attempting to solve problems involving human imponderables.

The two "aliens" aboard the ships also show a difference in the world-view of the two time periods in question. Spock represents the '80s ideal of a person who is responsible for his own actions. Worf, in contrast, shows the "go with the flow" sort of lifestyle that the '60s promoted. Worf wears a costume which is different from everyone else's, just as the hippies of the time wore beads, bangles and bracelets in order to express their individuality. Worf has long hair; definitely a '60s hallmark. Worf disregards orders, feeling that his own internal sense

of "honor" outweighs the regimentation of the "establishment." He's a free spirit but also comically outdated by today's standards.

DEPICTIONS OF PROGRESS

There was also the uglier side of the '60s, especially when it came to civil rights and the role of minorities. While today no one has any difficulty with the role of Uhura, the African-American communications officers, back in the '60s, before the strides in civil rights of the Martin Luther King Jr. era, it was felt that the only places for a "Negro" character was in the engine room, and that is where the pitiable LaForge is pent.

One must remember how benighted this era in our history was, and how shameful some of its excesses were. It was a time when blacks were segregated, oppressed, pushed aside and denied even the right to see and be seen. Poor LaForge is hidden away behind bars, bars which he carried around with him on his own face. His eyes are shielded, lest anyone feel "tainted" by the touch of his gaze. Thank goodness that this country has advanced away from this racist paranoia, and that now Uhura can take her place on the bridge, the equal of all the other characters.

On a far more optimistic note, New Trek certainly depicts the progress in medical science since the time of old Trek. Doctor McCoy, now, is able to cure just about anything, usually with no more effort than a wave of his mediscanner. In Old Trek, back in the '60s, poor Doctors Crusher and Pulaski had the most difficulty in curing even simple diseases or injuries. It is a shame that McCoy's modern skills in brain-transplant procedures couldn't have been around thirty years ago to save Tasha Yar from what was a fairly straightforward injury which, tragically, led to her death.

THE STANDARDS OF THE DAY

The point of this is that dramatic presentations do not exist in a vacuum. They must be seen against the backdrop of their times. It is pointless to watch a Shakespearean play without having some knowledge of the Elizabethan era in which Shakespeare labored. It is nonsensical to read Dickens or Melville without understanding the social and technological tumults that changed the world forever in the first half of the nineteenth century.

And it is completely unfair to judge STAR TREK, new and old, by the same standards, when the times have changed so drastically between the making of one and the other. To say that either is "better" than the other is, essentially, to ask if the future is "better" than the past.

The times they are a-changing, and if Kirk has some advantages over Picard, in all fairness we must point out that Picard was merely the product of a bygone era, whereas Kirk has the freshness of contemporaneity.

Perhaps in another thirty years, Kirk will seem as "dated" to us as Picard seems now. Perhaps, by then, however, we will be as charmed by him, through the actions of nostalgia on our memories as we now are charmed by the historical quaintness of Jean-Luc Picard.

JERRY SMITH, A TREK CLASSIC FAN, SPEAKS OUT

I am a huge fan of the original STAR TREK. Not every episode of the show was a gem, but the best shows are priceless classics which can be watched over and over without tiring. The movies have been touch and go, with II and IV being excellent and I and III being watchable.

When I first heard of ST—TNG, I couldn't wait to see it. I

thought, gee, here we have it, the chance for a perfect television show. Think of it: the groundwork for the STAR TREK universe had already been laid. Ensemble casting techniques had been totally redefined by such shows as HILL STREET BLUES and ST. ELSEWHERE, and 20 years had gone by—plenty of time to know what mistakes plagued the old show and how to avoid them.

I awaited ST—TNG with more than just an open mind. I eagerly looked forward to it. I didn't care that there was no Kirk or Spock; all I cared about was that my favorite TV show of all time was about to come back to the airwaves with original shows. How wrong I was.

ENCOUNTER AT LOW POINT

The premier of STAR TREK—THE NEXT GENERATION was probably the worst television show I ever watched of my own volition. The concept was confusing, the characters were dull, uninspired and lifeless, the acting was terrible and the captain was a total wimp.

I couldn't believe it. This was what 20 years of TV advancements had achieved? Impossible. Thinking it was just a two-hour fluke, I continued to watch, week after week,

until my fears were totally confirmed. ST—TNG was a failure. Here are a few of the reasons why.

THE NEW CREW: FIRST IMPRESSIONS

Jean Luc Picard: The wimpiest leader of anything in any medium I've ever seen. Gone were Captain Kirk's instant decisions and combat thinking, only to be replaced by Picard's gutless whining. He is incapable of making a decision without calling a two-hour conference and seeing what the ship's cook wants to do. He has surrendered the ship twice, an unforgivable act. No starship captain would ever do that in any century. The character is contemptible and not worthy of any respect from his crew. Picard is my biggest personal disappointment of the show.

Lt. Riker: A definite Captain Kirk clone and the only likable character on the show. If not for the terrible scripts, I believe this character would shine.

Dr. Crusher: She's cute, she's likable, she's leaving the show. It figures. Oh, well, she never would have fallen for a wimp like Picard anyway.

Deanna Troi: She would be all right if she just didn't shout her lines and didn't repeat every word she said. Remember the pilot?

"Captain Picard! Captain Picard! The pain! The pain!" Find some Excedrin honey. You've got headache #4051.

Geordi: This character seems to be okay, with some decent dialogue and the competent acting of LeVar Burton. Does anyone know why he wears banana clips over his eyes?

Data: The Spock clone. I've caught him stealing Spock's dialogue verbatim on several occasions. Why not just put another Vulcan on the show? I like Vulcans, and I'm not too fond of the Data character.

Wesley: The token child. I must admit I agree with Capt. Picard on one point. I don't like children on the bridge.

Worf: Having a Klingon on the Enterprise is an interesting idea. I just wish the show's scripts had fulfilled this promise. Nothing so far.

A PRISTINE FUTURE—TOO PRISTINE

I have nothing against the actors portraying the crew. On the contrary, I think they are a talented group of people. I especially like the actor who plays Capt. Picard. I just don't like his character on ST—TNG. The characters are just too perfect; they never get mad at each other. They never show signs of being human. There is no greed, hatred, prejudice; no vice to any of these characters.

I have a positive view of the future, but it's hard to imagine it being this rosy. Certain of the old Trek shows excelled at presenting human characters, people who had faults but were still likable human beings. I have yet to see a character on the new Trek I like half as much as anyone on the old.

The concepts of the new show are fine in theory, but extremely impractical when closely examined. Entire families on the Enterprise? Ridiculous. How many times in the original Trek was the ship threatened with destruction by some ultra-powerful madman? Once, twice a show? I can't believe Starfleet would take the chance of so many people from the same family being killed at once. Why would they want to send whole families into the unknown? I have never heard of families serving together on Navy ships, peacetime or not. This stretches my disbelief more than any other feature of the show.

The original STAR TREK has always been famous for its great villains. What happened to the Romulans? The Klingons on our side now? I wouldn't really mind the Klingons as Federation allies except for who they were replaced with—

two of the silliest antagonists ever on television. "Q"? It's hard to accept an all-powerful being who speaks with a lisp. The "Ferengi"? Oh, yeah, great replacement for the Klingons—fake-looking aliens who hop around like jackrabbits on acid. It would be like replacing Lex Luthor with a common street thug; no comparison and no class.

One thing I enjoy better than the original show is the special effects. Sometimes they look sort of fake (like the effects in a Saturday morning kid's show), but the space and planet effects are extremely well done.

To sum up, I would say that the entire ST—TNG series is as bad as the worst science fiction shows ever on television. Shows like SPACE: 1999, UFO and BUCK ROGERS had nothing to live up to. ST—TNG, however, has no excuse. The potential is there, but it has yet to be tapped.

IT'S ALWAYS SOMETHING

In spite of winning a Peabody Award for its twelfth episode, "The Big Goodbye," THE NEXT GENER- ATION still faced an uphill battle critically. TV GUIDE actually slammed "The Big Goodbye" as being a retread of the Trek Classic episode "A Piece of the Action,"

which it really wasn't. THE NEXT GENERATION did suffer from reworking old ground in other ways, though. "Datalore" was one of the most common of clichés—the evil twin, a concept used and reused by so many TV shows in the '70s that it had long since become a joke. When you see a TV episode which sounds like a comedy routine you've heard several times on LIVE FROM THE IMPROV, then you know that somebody is asleep at the switch.

The first year seemed to be tinged with desperation. "The Naked Now," a sequel to the Trek Classic episode "The Naked Time" was the third TNG episode aired. Doing that particular storyline that early in the first season has been criticized because we didn't really know what the normal characteriza- tions of the crew were like, so how could seeing them out of character have any effect? The fact of the matter is, "The Naked Time" was originally broadcast in 1966 as the fourth episode of the classic STAR TREK, and it worked. The reason it worked was because it revealed what was really inside these characters which therefore broadened our per- spective on Kirk, Spock and the oth- ers.

Somehow that didn't translate when "The Naked Now" was done. The inner self of these characters wasn't explored so much as they were shown to be just a little crazy. Wesley Crusher became a hopeless brat, which made us dislike him even more than we already did! And Tasha Yar, if anything, was just revealed to be horny for Data. Was that supposed to mean that she prefers having sex with robots than with real men? Was that her true inner self?

A STATE OF DENIAL

THE NEXT GENERATION did receive a lot of praise during its first season. This can be found by scanning the pages of the OFFICIAL STAR TREK FAN CLUB bulletin (which presented nothing but unqualified praise for TNG when it first aired) as well as in STARLOG. But at least STARLOG wasn't afraid to publish criticism.

STARLOG #127 (Feb. 1988) included the following comments on its letters pages.

J.R. HACKMAN: ". . . Cast your minds back a second, remember the animated STAR TREK? The strongest criticism was that most episodes were, in some way, remakes of the plots taken from the live series. Lastly, on THE NEXT GENERATION, I've seen remakes of several episodes of STAR TREK. They've done 'Squire of Gothos,' 'Naked Time,' 'Amok Time,' and 'Arena.' If I were paying for this show at a rate of $1 million an episode, I would take my plots from original material."

MIKE FACCIANI, JOHNSTOWN, PA: ". . . I'm not very impressed by STAR TREK—THE NEXT GENERATION. With all the hype, I expected it to be at least passable, but it can't even hold a candle to the real STAR TREK. To put it mildly, the new cast doesn't come off too well. They don't even have a fraction of the appeal that the original cast possessed and matters weren't helped by the two-hour premiere show, 'Encounter at Farpoint.' The story was boring and silly, but what's even worse was that the characters were also boring and silly!"

JOHN M. PETERS, NEVADA CITY, CA: ". . . I was thrilled by the visual beauty of ST—TNG, but in terms of story, characters and relationships, it certainly fell short of the quality of the original STAR TREK pilots, 'The Cage/Menagerie' and 'Where No Man Has Gone Before.' I would have loved a story that purely explored relationships including family life aboard the Enterprise and gave a nice background on all the principal characters with possibly a little minor action adventure on the side as a subplot. Remember that wonderful 'bar tender' scene between Captain Pike (Jeffrey Hunter) and his doctor (John Hoyt) in 'The Menagerie'? It instantly made you care about the characters you had just met."

THE KLINGONS FEARED THEM?!

There were also letters from fans who really liked what they'd seen on THE NEXT GENERATION, but at least STARLOG was willing to publish contrary points of view along side them. I think that TNG had been on a couple of years before the official STAR TREK fan club let any letters be published which were less than salutary.

STARLOG #130 (April 1988) featured a letter regarding the Ferengi, which voiced the complaints of many.

TERESA BURQUIST, S. PASADENA, CA: ". . . The biggest disappointment of all are the Ferengi. We are supposed to believe that they are more fierce than the Klingons. This is, after all, why the Klingons joined the Federation in the first place! When we are finally introduced to the Ferengi in 'The Last Outpost," they act like bungling idiots and monkeys. The Klingons were something to be feared, with or without their technology. The Ferengi are supposed to

have technology equal to that of the Federation. And we are to believe that they are more fierce than the Klingons?"

That gives you a pretty good idea of how some people responded to STAR TREK—THE NEXT GENERATION during its first couple of seasons and that there were clearly some souls who were less than impressed.

MODERN TIMES

Flashing forward 5 years, even though TNG has been embraced by most STAR TREK fans, not everyone remains thrilled. In STARLOG #194 (September 1993) a writer offered some modner criticism.

MATT ISGRIG, ARNOLD, MO: ". . . I think the sixth season is campy. I mean, the plots have been good—for Saturday morning cartoons—but as episodes of what TV GUIDE called 'TV's most-improved series,' they just don't cut it. If the Enterprise could survive the Borg, how was it crippled and taken over by a handful of Ferengi in 'Rascals'? Where were all the security personnel? 'Starship Mine' introduced a character who was interesting because he was so boring!

Strangely enough, that character was killed off minutes later and nothing was ever said about him.

The two-part episode 'Birthright' should have been only one part, and what became of Data's story in the second half? Why was he having those dreams? If the season really needed another two-parter after the already much-criticized 'Chains of Command,' then it should have been 'Relics,' because that episode in which Scotty appeared seemed cramped for time and space. It involved a Dyson Sphere, which is supposedly as big around as our entire solar system, yet the Enterprise flew right around it and found the stranded Scotty! Also, what's with all this ending the episodes with the characters laughing or in humorous situations?"

Whether you agree with the criticisms or not, at least it shows that people are watching and care enough to say what they think. Unfortunately criticism you dislike is easy to dismiss when you take into account the fact that there are fans out there who actually liked the recent science fiction stinker SPACE RANGERS on CBS and they wrote in to tell STARLOG about that, too. So when it comes to criticism, you have to analyze what is being said and decide if there's any validity to the claims. This is particularly interesting to do now when even the fans of TNG tend to agree that the first season was pretty weak, while at the time many of them thought it was just wonderful. It all comes down to perspective, and sometimes to hindsight when we have something better to compare it with.

A mixed bag of classics and disappointments in spite of Rick Berman's determination to outdo season five. He didn't quite make it.

The sixth season of STAR TREK-THE NEXT GENERATION had its ups and downs. It kicked off with the disastrous "Time's Arrow, Part Two," a shambles of a tale (scripted by Jeri Taylor from a "story" by Joe Menosky) that revealed the complete lack of foresight involved in the first half of the plot. The writers clearly had no idea of how they were going to resolve the situations set up in Part One. No better solution to the dilemma of Data's severed head could be found than to reconnect it to his body after spending five centuries in a subterranean cavern; no better examination of the late eighteenth century could be devised than to dredge up Samuel Clemens— probably the most obvious choice— as the episode's historical celebrity, then set him loose on the Enterprise, where he

takes up an inordinate amount of screen time spouting spurious Twainisms in a futile effort to plug a few of the holes in the threadbare plot of "Time's Arrow." No questions about Guinan were really answered. And worse, no interesting new questions about her were to be found in this weary excuse for a season opener.

THE NEXT GENERATION veered back into a comfortable mediocrity with "Realm of Fear," the weakest of the three Barclay stories to date. Still enlivened by the ever-engaging performance of A-TEAM veteran Dwight Schultz. This Brannon Braga scripted episode (directed by Cliff Bole) found Barclay back in the focus, having anxiety attacks about using the transporter and finding strange creatures in the matter stream when he finally takes the plunge.

Winrich Kolbe directed "Man Of The People," writer Frank Abetamarco's 24th-century take on Oscar Wilde's THE PORTRAIT OF DORIAN GREY, aided by some serious rewriting by committee, in which Ambassador Alkar of Lumeria is revealed as a master manipulator who gains his strength in negotiations by depositing his negative emotions in some hapless victim for the duration. He winds up forcefully charming, and always successful; his victim begins to age rapidly, and dies.

This time around, his victim is Deanna Troi, who (for some reason) becomes oversexed before going crazy and senile. Pointless, but great fun for all fans of Marina

David Warner and his wife attending a movie premiere in West Hollywood.

Photo © 1993 Albert L. Ortega

Sirtis' physique, which is displayed to full advantage in numerous scenes. But this whole setting aside of the emotions in a living receptacle— didn't Sarek do that to Picard in the third season? Same idea, different results.

ALL THIS, AND SCOTTY, TOO

The next episode, "Relics," featured the return of James Doohan as lovable engineer Montgomery Scott. In Ron Moore's script, it seems that a ship with Scotty on board crashed in a remote region of space, and he rigged a feedback cycle in the transporter which kept his transporter pattern intact for seventy years or more. Some amusing moments as Scotty's earnest attempts to help out start to get on Geordi's nerves. But there's no surprise when the two engineers team up and find the solution to the latest threat to the Enterprise. Director Alexander Singer pulled off this potentially schmaltzy hour with great aplomb, utilizing some real special effects wizardry to re-create the bridge of Jim Kirk's Enterprise in one movingly nostalgic scene.

Best moment: Scotty's incredulity upon discovering that when the captain asks how long a repair will take, Geordi tells him exactly how long it really will take, instead of inflating the time required. (Who hasn't suspected that this was Scotty's ploy all along?)

Most glaring omission: Scotty is taken aback to discover how much time has elapsed, but he doesn't even ask what has happened to any of his former crew mates. Some of them must be dead— or can we anticipate eventually finding everyone who ever appeared on STAR TREK trapped in some sort of time suspension? Let's hope not!

CAT POEMS AND SECRET Qs

Directed by Robert Wiemer, "Schisms" brought a welcome dose of drama and fear into the sixth season. It's not a classic, but an overdue bit of tension nevertheless. The best part is the opening sequence, largely unrelated to the main plot, in which Data recites a poem he has written in honor of his faithful cat, Spot. But Commander Riker's lack of attention here is due less to the dullness of Data's creative writing than it does to the fact that he's being abducted nightly by aliens who are performing nasty experiments on him and on other hapless members of the Enterprise crew. Riker must piece together this mystery and stay awake to save the day. The whole problem, it seems, was made possible by an unforeseen side effect of an experiment cooked up by Geordi LaForge. Lots of technospeak in this Brannon Braga script (from a story by Ronald Wilkerson and Jean Mathias), but still an intriguing effort.

As the title might suggest, "True Q" brings back John DeLancie yet again to bedevil Jean-Luc Picard. The story here, scripted by Rene Echevarria and directed by Robert Scherrer, was inspired by a submission by a high school student who envisioned a tale (perhaps predictably) in which a teenager discovers that he is a member of the race known only as Q, with all its attendant powers. This was recrafted to feature a young Enterprise intern named Amanda (the gorgeous Olivia D'Abo) whose parents were, unbeknownst to her, Q who had renounced their powers to live on Earth as humans. Their death in an accident, years earlier, is revealed as an out-and-out murder by the Q, and the Q we know and hate is really on hand with a deadly mission: he must kill Amanda if it is necessary. But he offers her a choice: renounce her powers and live as a human, or rejoin the Q completely. The third option is death. Typically, Q tests her resolve to remain human by tempting her to explore her power, much to Picard's everlasting chagrin.

KIDS IN SPACE

In the following episode, "Rascals," Picard, Guinan, Ensign Ro and Keiko (Mrs. O'Brien, to Miles) are caught in a transporter accident (this season's favorite plot device, the transporter) and return as children— obviously a fifth season story held over a year. Mentally, they're still adults, but Picard soon relieves himself of duty and hands command over to Riker due to the peculiar nature of his affliction. No sooner is this done than the Enterprise is taken over by Ferengi pirates in stolen Klingon vessels. Among other things, they herd all the children together as hostages— including the victims of the transporter snafu. Picard uses his adult wits and his junior stature to outwit the Ferengi, recruiting Alexander (a.k.a. Worf Junior) into the plot. Directed by Adam Nimoy from a script by Allison Hock; story by Ward Botsford, Diane Dru Botsford and Michael Piller. Piller should have known better. This is about as close as NEXT GENERATION has ever come to doing the kind of humorous, tongue-in-cheek episodes which classic Trek did during its second season.

SHOOTOUT ON NCC-1701-D

"A Fistful of Datas." Think about it minute. Savor the title. A lot of thought went into it. And it's funny, since this is a Western. Yes, a

Western. Must be a holodeck story, right? Right. Worf and Alexander undertake a gunslinging adventure in the Old West, and are joined by Deanna, a real fun outing. Until, if you can believe it, something goes wrong with the holodeck. And since the problem is caused by an experimental linkage between the ship's computer and Data's brain, all the bad guys in this simulated cowboy adventure (scripted by Robert Hewitt Wolfe and Brannon Braga from Wolfe's script) wind up looking like Data. Look back at that title again. It's probably the best thing about this profoundly silly episode. Directed, embarrassingly enough, by Patrick Stewart. This was apparently supposed to be funny, too. I'm sure it was on the set. I'd love to see the out-takes.

Data champions a new electronic life form in the Jonathan Frakes-directed episode "Quality Of Life." It involves small robotic tools that seem, to Data, to have developed sentience, unbeknownst even to their creator, Dr. Faralon. She and the others don't buy into Data's arguments that the "exocomps" are alive, and when it seems that the exocomps must be destroyed, Data violates orders so that he can protect them.

A good, engaging follow-up to the earlier "The Measure of A Man," "Quality of Life" may not be one of the greatest Data stories ever, but it was one of the best episodes of this season up to this point despite the weaknesses of science consultant Naren Shankar's first script; the mere fact that Data is the focus always gives Brent Spiner plenty of opportunities to explore his character in greater depth than usual.

CARDASSIAN TORTURE GARDEN

The drama in STAR TREK— THE NEXT GENERATION finally took a darker turn in the two-parter "Chain of Command." The first part, scripted by Ron Moore from a story by Frank Abetemarco, kicks off with Picard, Crusher and Worf undertaking a secret intelligence gathering mission against the Cardassians. This poses a problem. After all this talk of the Prime Directive most of the time, the Federation turns around and sends a team out on a covert mission, much as they did in "Unification." And the fact that they send Picard on the mission really stretches the credulity a bit, too. Wouldn't they have people trained for specific jobs like this, so they won't have to pull key personnel off of an important Starfleet vessel?

Logic falls by the wayside early in this outing. But all this is simply a buildup to the central focus of the twinned episodes: Picard's duel of wills with the torturing Cardassian officer, Gul Madred (David Warner). The first part also introduces Captain Jellico (Ronnie Cox), Picard's (permanent?) replacement on board the Enterprise, an overbearing lout who alienates everybody, especially Riker. One note: although this show was timed to coincide with the debut of DEEP SPACE NINE, it only used the new show as a distant backdrop. Originally, the secret mission would have actually taken the spy team through DS-9, where Beverly Crusher would charm Quark into helping them gain passage into Cardassian space. When this idea was scrapped, a different Ferengi (created with a simple name change) took over Quark's dialogue. Able direction was provided by Robert Scheerer.

The second part, scripted by Abetemarco alone and directed by Les Landau, opens with Picard securely in Cardassian custody, face to face with Gul Madred. This was a real cost-saver, as it took place in one room with no special effects beyond a few lights which featured prominently in Madred's vicious assaults on Picard's body and dignity. Meanwhile, Captain Jellico steered the Enterprise into real jeopardy while trying to outguess Cardassian military strategy, and nearly gets in over his head.

This scenario, like the Picard/Madred torture drama, is undercut considerably by the sudden resolution created by the Cardassians' abrupt withdrawal from Bajor and their new treaty with the Federation. But Patrick Stewart and David Warner really pulled off their play-within-a-play, while Ronnie Cox was also great in the somewhat hamstrung subplot. Any way you look at it, "Chain of Command" showed that despite such contrivances as the espionage subplot, THE NEXT GENERATION could still make them like it used to, or better.

MORE MORIARTY

Rene Echevarria's "Ship In A Bottle," directed by Alexander Singer, dips deep into the back history of THE NEXT GENERATION and brings back a character all but forgotten: the holodeck's first sentient creation, Professor Moriarty, left hanging in the computer memory way back in "Elementary, Dear Data." Somehow, Moriarty manages to make his way back into the holodeck, somehow achieving consciousness while in storage, and emerging to confront Ensign Barclay (Dwight Schultz) with his tale of woe. (Shouldn't Barclay be in a twelve-step program for holodeck addicts by now?)

Moriarty is keen on having Picard keep his promise to release him, if possible, and seems a quite reasonable character until he takes over the ship! It takes Picard a while to figure out that Moriarty only has control of the holodeck, but has tricked Picard into accepting the simulation as real. Picard turns the tables by escaping and finally giving Moriarty what he wants: releasing him, with his holographic paramour, in a small spacecraft to roam the galaxies. Of course, this, in turn, is a holodeck program, isolated from the rest of the ship's computer's. It will be a long time before Moriarty has any reason to suspect that he's been had!

DOGS IN SPACE (ROMULANS, TOO)

"Aquiel" places Geordi in a dual mystery/romance scripted by Brannon Braga and Ron Moore, from a story by Jeri Taylor; the redoubtable Cliff Bole directed. Unfortunately for Geordi, his romance with the title character, a beautiful woman on an isolated science station, is undermined by the suspicion that she may have murdered the only other person on the station in a most unpleasant fashion.

Eventually, it turns out that some sort of evil shape shifting alien is behind the killing. Could Aquiel be this alien? The only other entity on the station is her dog— yet nobody has the presence of mind to suspect that the alien may be hiding in canine form until it reveals itself and almost kills Geordi, long after the audience has figured out that the dog did it.

Naren Shankar fares better with his script for "Face Of The Enemy," a fun, if cheesy, episode (directed by Gabrielle Beaumont) that brings back memories of "The Enterprise Incident." In a great introduction, Deanna Troi wakes up feeling a bit out of it, and rightly so. She's been taken aboard a Romulan ship and been altered to look like a Romulan. The reason: several important members of the Romulan underground (as seen in the fifth season episodes "Unification I" and "Unification II") plan to defect, and are being smuggled in suspended animation by sympathizers among the Romulan crew. But this secret mission will not get by the watchful Commander Toreth unless Deanna can successfully impersonate a member of the Romulan secret police. Unfortunately, Toreth is not a typical Romulan, and resents this impingement on her command more than she fears it, which makes Deanna's job all that much harder. It's cat-fight heaven as the two women size each other up and engage in a battle of wills.

Apparently, some thought is even being given to the notion of bringing back Commander Toreth. And in a side note, some of the writers toyed with the twisted idea of having one of the defectors turn out to be Spock— only to have his suspension unit fail, killing him! This idea did not get very far, needless to say.

IT'S A WONDERFUL Q

It's bad news for Picard when he dies and has a classic afterlife experience with one alarming variation. Q is there, with the disturbing information that he is god. The episode is entitled "Tapestry," making it the only Q episode since "Encounter At Farpoint" that does not have the letter "Q" in the title. Feigning benevolence, Q gives Picard a chance to relive a crucial episode of his youth. The bar fight, recounted to Wesley Crusher a few years back, that led to Picard's need for an artificial heart. Thanks to Ron Moore's script and Winrich

Kolbe's astute direction, this is more than a mere IT'S A WONDERFUL LIFE rehash, but a truly revealing insight into the past of Jean-Luc Picard, highlighting the differences between the brash youth and the mature leader of men. And Q is a bit more serious than usual here, not a comic relief character. John DeLancie brings the usual touches of malevolent wit to Q's comings and goings.

DATA'S DREAMS, WORF'S NIGHTMARE

Originally a one part story, "Birthright" was eventually expanded into a double episode when it became clear that Brannon Braga's main story, detailing Worf's search for his father in a Romulan prison camp, needed more time to be told adequately. It did not, however, warrant a full two hours to itself, which led to the creation of a secondary story line, thematically related to the Worf plot, to fill out the first half of the episode. This, ironically, became far more interesting than the main plot, and certainly more so than that plot's resolution in the second half.

"Birthright I," directed by Winrich Kolbe, takes the Enterprise to Deep Space Nine, where Dr. Julian Bashir has a strange alien device from the Gamma Quadrant that needs examination. A power surge from this artifact knocks Data out of commission. While he is "off," he has a vision of his creator, Dr. Noonian Soong, replete with mysterious imagery.

Meanwhile, an alien on DS-9's Promenade has told Worf that his father is still alive. Worf dismisses this idea, but when he learns of Data's vision, he realizes that he must investigate. While Worf begins his mission, Data tries to explore his subconscious, if he has one, and eventually discovers that Soong had programmed him with the ability to dream, an ability that would have been activated at the proper stage of Data's development if the power surge hadn't kicked it in prematurely. A knock-off idea, perhaps, but really a crucial stage in the saga of Data, this subplot is memorable for its dream sequences and its scenes of Data's driven efforts to examine his newfound dream imagery through a succession of paintings.

The Data plotline was resolved in "Birthright I." "Birthright II" (written by Echevarria and directed by effects maestro Dan Curry) followed Worf's mission to its conclusion as he finds that his father is, in fact, dead. But the survivors of Khitomer are still alive, living in the Romulan camp. In this backwater of the Romulan empire, Klingon/Romulan relations are more cordial (although still harsh) than Worf had expected, and he sets about instructing the younger Klingons, born in the camp, about the glories of Klingon culture. Unfortunately, this becomes a bit predictable, culminating in scenes of the sort that always remind this writer of Rod Taylor's efforts to rouse the Eloi to battle in George Pal's THE TIME MACHINE. Even so, the episode has a lot going for it, with ambiguities and ironies abounding throughout.

PICARD KICKS SOME AND GETS SOME

After all this thought-provoking material in the past few episodes, "Starship Mine" came as a breath of fresh air: an out-an-out action episode, scripted by newcomer Morgan Gendel and directed by Cliff Bole. When the Enterprise is emptied for maintenance, Picard and his main officers find themselves trapped at a planetside reception dominated by the most aggressively boring officer in Starfleet.

While this gives Data a welcome chance to practice the human art of small talk, Picard takes the first excuse that presents itself to leave, returning to his ship to get something important. He stumbles into a plot to steal dangerous material from the Enterprise, and must combat the mercenaries behind it. Obviously, it's DIE HARD on the Enterprise, but it's good, straight-ahead fun, so who's complaining?

After all the episodes in which Picard ran around with younger women (not many, but they were always younger women), "Lessons" finally has the good Captain find romance with a woman his own age; his match in maturity, experience and dedication. Since Nella Darren (Wendy Hughes) is also a scientist, there are bound to be career conflicts. This is a thoughtful character-driven piece with a weak crisis interjected near the end, highlighted by Picard's discussion of his experience in "Inner Light" the previous season. "Lessons" was scripted by Ronald Wilkerson and Jean Louise Mathias, and directed by Robert Weimer.

FORWARD INTO THE PAST

Picard's past resurfaces once more in "The Chase," when his old archaeology professor Richard Galen (Norman Lloyd) appears and offers him a chance to help him discover one of the greatest archaeological mysteries of all the ages. Picard is tempted but inevitably, he cannot leave the Enterprise behind. But when Galen's transport is attacked, it becomes apparent that the secrets he had been hinting at were far more volatile than Picard had suspected. When the Professor dies of severe disruptor injuries, Picard takes up the trail, which is also being followed by Cardassians, Klingons, and those sneaky Romulans who show up at the last minute.

The plot hinges on a real MacGuffin. It seems that some sort of information has been encoded on the DNA of various worlds. Put the last piece together and a four-billion year old message reveals the worm-eaten science fiction concept that sentient life was seeded throughout space by some ancient humanoid race. The chase is more intriguing than the denouement, a sentiment echoed by the non-human participants, who had hoped for some sort of weapon. This sort of stands as an ultimately heavy-handed restatement of the classic STAR TREK message of universal love and unity. This tale, directed by Jonathan Frakes, is scripted by Joe Menosky from a story by Menosky and Ronald D. Moore.

EVERYTHING'S MELTING

The spirit of Philip K. Dick invades THE NEXT GENERATION

in "Frame Of Mind," a mind-bending episode that recalls such reality-twisting Dick classics such as UBIK and A MAZE OF DEATH more than his best known work DO ANDROIDS DREAM OF ELECTRIC SHEEP? (better known in its movie version, BLADERUNNER). A classic Brannon Braga script, directed by Jim Conway, finds Will Riker taking part in a play directed by Enterprise drama coach Beverly Crusher. It's about a mental patient's struggle to retain his dignity. But reality is not what it seems. Riker really is in an alien mental institution, where he is subjected to constant reality flips. Is he in the play imagining it is real, or is the reality something else entirely? Great effects show reality shattering like a mirror as Riker struggles to regain his bearings. A strong performance by Jonathan Frakes carries one of the best sixth season episodes.

"Suspicions" recasts Beverly Crusher as Quincy-in-space, trying to find the solution to the apparent murder of an alien scientist. It's pretty obvious early on that the death is faked, so the big surprise really isn't one, although we do get to see Crusher defend herself quite effectively (watch it— she fights dirty, guys!). At least Guinan is on hand, and one character, a Ferengi scientist, at least reveals that there is a little bit more to the Ferengi stereotype than we usually see. Menosky and Shankar scripted; Cliff Bole directed.

KLINGON RESURRECTION

"Rightful Heir" revives an ancient Klingon warrior who has taken on certain messianic qualities in the Klingon religion, provoking a crisis for Worf and the Klingon Empire alike. Kehless (seen as one of history's most "evil" people in the old STAR TREK episode "The Savage Curtain") is a charismatic but obstinate fellow with grandiose ideas of ruling the Empire, backed by a cadre of priests. Is he a fake? Gowron, threatened by this resurrection, would certainly like to think so.

But everything, including DNA samples from bloodstains on an ancient relic, would seem to indicate that Kehless is the real McCoy (pardon the expression). But those bloodstains hold the truth: the priests have cloned Kehless, who really thinks that he's the original! An intriguing story, like most Klingon episodes, that raises some fascinating ambiguities. Kevin Conway turns in a moving and effective performance as the ultimately baffled Kehless. Winrich

Kolbe directed from the writing of James E. Brooks as scripted by Ronald D. Moore.

DOUBLE YOUR RIKERS, OR. . .

"Second Chances" is the second strong Riker outing in the sixth season, giving Jonathan Frakes another lead role. A freak transporter anomaly eight years earlier got Riker off a dangerous planet just in the nick of time. But a refracted transporter beam also beamed a duplicate back down, leaving him to survive until the Enterprise arrives to reclaim some scientific data. Both Rikers are faced with what their lives would have been like if they had made different choices. The "new" Lieutenant Riker still carries a torch for Deanna. And Commander Riker is more than slightly rankled when his counterpart actually gets into Deanna's pants!

This is a well-done episode that avoids clichés: the "other" Riker is not an evil twin, but a person with as much claim to his identity as the "regular" Riker. He also survives the episode— what need was there to kill him off, after all? Actually, the staff writers toyed with the idea of killing off the "regular" Riker, which would have been a real show-stopper! This marked LeVar Burton's directorial debut, working from Michael Medlock's story as scripted by Rene Echevarria.

Son-of-Spock, Adam Nimoy, returned to direct "Timescape," from a complicated script by Brannon Braga that chokes on its own convoluted premise. It does, however, get off to a rousing start. Romulans, mysterious aliens, and the apparent death of several key Enterprise officers all add up to this fascinating but ultimately mixed blessing of an episode.

THE BEGINNING OF THE END. . .

It's another season-closing cliffhanger in "Descent," a Ron Moore/Jeri Taylor story which brings back the Borg after a season-long absence. It's also predominantly a Data story, effectively bookending the season with dramas centering on the affable android. And in this Alexander Singer directed outing, Data's going through some changes again. And so have the Borg: no longer are they units of a hive mentality bent on assimilation; they are, instead, ruthless battle warriors with individual personalities and a sense of themselves and other Borg as discrete entities.

But before the action gets underway, "Descent" opens with Data playing poker on the holodeck with three great physicists; Isaac Newton (played by John Neville, star of Terry Gilliam's ADVENTURES OF BARON MUNCHAUSEN), Albert Einstein (Jim Norton) and Stephen Hawking (played by himself). The Borg threat leads to a firefight in which Data experiences emotion at killing one of the Borg. Disturbingly, he enjoys it. This aside, the Enterprise command team is perplexed by the change in the Borg. Could Hugh, the Borg encountered in "I, Borg," have something to do with this transformation? And why are they so vicious?

When Data disappears in a shuttle craft, the game is truly afoot, and the Enterprise traces him to a distant planet. He is found in a strange building, where the Away Team, including Picard, is suddenly surrounded by angry Borg. Data appears above them, apparently the leader of the Borg— but it is not Data, but his evil brother, Lore. Data's appearance at Lore's side is the final twist in this episode: the twins seem to have joined forces, and are intent on destroying the Federation!

This is clearly the set-up for a real smash-'em-up finale. The only question is— will THE NEXT GENERATION's writers pull it off, or will they fall flat on their faces again as they did with "Time's Arrow II"? Odds are they learned their lesson last time. But with the seventh season production schedule moved forward a month this year, it would help if they had had some sort of resolution in mind when they wrote the set up. As for the sixth season— it was the best of seasons, it was (almost) the worst of seasons, a year of inconsistent quality whose best hours seem to balance out the duds. One more year to go. Let's hope it's a good one!

Chapter Five
SAREK OF VULCAN

Sarek, the father of Spock, is the son of Skor and Solkar, one of the wealthiest and most revered families on Vulcan. In his lifetime, he has become one of the most respected men in the galaxy.

As a child he performed, and excelled in the rituals that were expected of all Vulcan children. He obeyed his father without question, and was betrothed at the age of seven to a Vulcan princess. After entering school he followed in his father's footsteps and began studies that would lead to a career in his world's diplomatic corps.

When he reached the proper age, he married his Vulcan princess and eventually a son, Sybok, was born. However, his delight at having a son was clouded by the death of his young wife.

With the help of family members he began to train the boy in the Vulcan customs of families of his stature, but Sybok rebelled early. When Sarek was appointed as the first Vulcan Ambassador to planet Earth, he believed it would be in the child's best interests to leave him in the care of the Old Masters on the high plateau of Gol.

SAREK AND AMANDA

It would be five years before Sarek returned to Vulcan. But to his father's distress he brought a human wife, the former Amanda Grayson. Sarek wasn't breaking any rules with his second marriage, for according to Vulcan law, when a spouse dies, the survivor may find a new mate of their choice. A Vulcan had never previously married a human and Skor was disappointed that his son was the first. Perhaps he was afraid the new wife would lead him from the Vulcan ways, but in that he was wrong.

The couple brought Sybok home and Amanda was drawn to the boy at once, but he didn't respond. He was rude and disrespectful, forcing Sarek to return the boy to the Masters for further instructions in the disciplines expected of male children.

Sybok promised he'd improve his behavior if allowed to remain at home but made the mistake of saying he thought the Masters were wrong, and he wanted to be free to think as he chose.

SPOCK AS A YOUTH

When Spock was born, Sarek vowed not to make the same mistakes with this son as he had with the first. The only problem was he had no idea what those mistakes were.

Sybok made infrequent visits to his family home, but when he came, he tried to instill in his younger half brother some of his own beliefs. But Spock would accept nothing Sybok tried to tell him.

Spock was having his own problems. The other children would tease him because he was half human, and Spock would try even harder to be the perfect Vulcan child. When Spock was twelve, Sybok ran away from Vulcan with a group of his like-thinking friends. Many years would pass before the two would meet again, and then under circumstances neither could have imagined.

Whatever emotion Sarek felt about the defection of his first born was skillfully concealed, but Sybok's name was never mentioned in the household again. Despite Amanda's pleas that he was just a boy, Sarek continued to pressure Spock to do better. But he couldn't. In a desperate attempt to learn more about the human side of himself, to discover a way to purge what he considered a weakness (but against his father's wishes), Spock applied to, and was accepted at, Starfleet Academy.

RECONCILIATION

Sarek again disowned a son. Amanda began to wonder how this man she loved, who was so gentle and understanding with her, could not accept that sons sometimes needed understanding and, yes, even a little gentleness as well.

"Will he ever mellow; become just a little less Vulcan?" she would wonder. The thought never occurred to her that eighteen years would pass before father and son would again communicate with each other or become reconciled.

Perhaps some ancient Vulcan god intervened for the reunion transpired on the Enterprise. Sarek was one of a group of ambassadors being transported to a secret location code-named Babel, to determine if the world of Coridan should be admitted to the Federation.

Sarek became ill, and only a blood transfusion would save him. Spock was the one being on board with compatible blood. The transfusion was a success, and thus began the first tiny crack in the mellowing that Amanda had spent years hoping would happen. She did, however, feel like shaking him at his reply, when she suggested he thank his son for saving his life.

"Spock behaved in the only logical manner open to him. One does not thank logic, Amanda."

This event transpired at about the mid-point in Sarek's life. He and Spock became much more congenial, and carried on what were sometimes heated conversations during the rare times they should meet, each trying to explain something in their own particular logic.

SAREK'S CONFESSION

It would not be until Spock's death and rebirth that Sarek allowed his emotions to surface for all to see.

"My logic falters. . . where my son is concerned," was Sarek's reply when T'Lar explained that the fal-tor-pan he had requested for Spock was not logical.

It may be true that nearly losing a son would cause even a Vulcan to lose emotional control, but Sarek was trained for that possibility. What was not included in his training? How to react to those illogical people from Earth.

What Sarek had to learn to understand was the emotion that prompted Kirk and his officers to risk everything, their lives, their careers, perhaps even their freedom, to do such an illogical thing as to steal a starship. Then use it to go charging off into space to rescue the essence of a fellow being when they had no real assurance that he was still alive, or that they could even locate his body to return to a grieving father.

This single act of high-powered emotionalism in the twenty-third century had much to do with Sarek's growth as an effective mediator in the twenty-fourth century.

STRUCK DOWN

Effective as he'd been in the early part of his career, many believe his greatest achievements came in the last third of his life—after he had learned a little properly used emotion can be an effective tool when negotiating with adversaries.

Although the reason has not yet been recorded, somewhere between the death of Amanda and the marriage of Sarek to his third wife, Perrin, the Vulcan ambassador and his son, Spock, suffered another period of estrangement. Some feel that Perrin was behind it as she and Spock did not get along. For this reason Spock was not summoned to Sarek's side when his father became ill.

Ben Dye's disease is a rare affliction which strikes only Vulcans, and then only very few Vulcans ever fall victim to it. The disease affects a Vulcan's emotional centers of the brain, causing them to lose their rigid control in spite of a century or more of self-discipline. The stricken Vulcan even mentally projects their emotions, which other people detect peripherally, and this can cause shortness of temper and other emotional outbursts among innocent bystanders.

Sarek started manifesting serious symptoms during a diplomatic mission aboard the Enterprise-D. Only by mind-melding with Jean-Luc Picard was Sarek able to maintain his composure and complete his negotiations aboard the Enterprise.

THE END OF A BRILLIANT LIFE

Several months later, with Sarek even more gravely ill, the Federation learned that Spock had secretly gone to Romulus. Since Spock was on no official diplomatic mission there was speculation that Spock was defecting. Captain Picard visited Sarek and during moments of clarity the Vulcan expressed no knowledge of Spock's mission, although he was aware of a Romulan ambassador Spock had met with officially before.

Sarek melded with Picard one last time and gave him a message for Spock as Sarek and his son had never mind-melded.

When Sarek died of Ben Dye's disease at the age of 203, not only Vulcan and the Federation lost a great force for good, but the entire galaxy.

The 23rd and 24th centuries have seen the discovery of a number of alien races as well as radical changes in the way some of them deal with the Federation.

"... to explore strange new worlds, to seek out new life and new civilizations..."

The dictionary definition of aliens describes them as "... foreign, strange, a being from outer space..." When do they cease to be alien? When they become fellow-travelers, friends, companions, shipmates and fellow workers? How do they compare to each other?

Perhaps most important, why are the aliens different in the 23rd century than those of the 24th? How do the species of one century compare with those from another? Why do some disappear after one contact, while other, unknown life forms suddenly make themselves known?

Chapter Six
THE SECRET ORIGINS OF THE MAJOR ALIEN RACES OF STAR TREK

VULCANS

Vulcans have been known to the inhabitants of Earth since the earliest days of Earth's space exploration. They have long served side-by-side with humans and are Earth's most enduring ally.

The planet now referred to as Vulcan was formed in the 40 Eridani stellar system some 8 billion years ago. Earth is believed to be 60 million years younger than Vulcan. The star system contains three stellar bodies. These consist of a white giant primary and two lesser stars, an orange yellow and another lesser golden star. It is a true triple star system. The white giant's gravity well forced the larger orange-yellow into a hyperdense white dwarf. The lesser golden star became a diffuse red dwarf.

The two dwarfs rotate each other in an inverse angle to the white giant. Therefore the gravity well for the entire system lies in a spot between the three stars. This is similar to the Sol System's twin planet combination, Pluto and Charon. A center of gravity exists in the space between the tumbling balls of ice, rock and methane. This graviton center would lead to an unusual climate shift in Vulcan that would change life there forever.

VULCAN HISTORY

The four smaller planets which formed have compositions that allowed for the creation of life. The inner three were too hot and 40 Eri A-IV (Vulcan) was too cold to allow for the basic chemistry to begin. The dust cloud that formed Vulcan developed into a rare double planet orbit with a gravity center away from the planet, exactly like Sol's Pluto/Charon system. The moon was named T'Khut by the Vulcans. That translates roughly as "The Watcher."

Terran astronomers call the second planet entwined with Vulcan's orbit "Charis" after the cheerful goddess, one of the three Graces, who married the jilted god of the forge when Vulcan was forsaken by the goddess Love, who chose War. Vulcans have several names for their planet including at least one known only to Vulcans. Life primarily evolved along copper based lines, as opposed to Terra's iron based beings. That explains why Vulcan blood is green and Terran blood red when exposed to a nitrogen/oxygen atmosphere.

Vulcans developed in an idyllic Eden, or Shake Re, a beautiful world full of giant trees and abundant water supplies. Life flourished until an apparent solar event led to a massive increase in heat and radiation from the primary white giant. The trees burned, the water dried up and Vulcan became the desert land that exists to this day. Giant creatures lived under the sand in the prehistoric days and their appearance has continued, including one notable event in the life of a young Vulcan named Surak, who will have more effect on the planet than any being before or after his birth.

But there were millennia of Vulcan history before Surak came into play. It is often misunderstood among humans who believe that the pointy-eared green-skinned beings have no emotions. Nothing could be further from the truth. Vulcan emotions are a very intense form and Vulcans strive to master their emotions.

A CULTURE OF EXCLUSION

Vulcan society evolved into a xenophobic planet by necessity. The first contact with alien life came when pirates arrived to loot the planet. That disastrous first contact led to centuries of isolation and sponsored generations of mistrust. That first contact is also the reason the Wanderers left to found a new world. Those wanderers are commonly referred to as the Romulans.

The attack on Vulcan was the touchstone in Romulan history and their isolationist policy is based on that one attack millennia ago. More information can be found in the Romulan's own separate file. Surak's finest student led the group that lived at relativistic speeds for years at a time. That is why Vulcan culture evolved for centuries while the Romulan culture evolved on ships in a matter of decades.

Vulcan funded the program to get Surak's opponents away before Vulcan reverted to the ancient ways. The Wanderers supported the government action since they did not want to bankrupt their progenitor planet. Vulcan culture is still the root of Romulan culture. However, neither would consider it logical.

Vulcans developed extra senses as generations of tribes used their genetic traits to trade up in power and possibility. For example, the Tribe of the Eye had a second eyelid that allowed their warriors to see in daylight, giving them a strategic advantage over their adversaries. They intermarried with another tribe that possessed powers of psi, such as mindmelding. That allows hundreds of thousands of Vulcans to trace their family along specific lines to specific tribes.

SURAK AND THE MENTAL ARTS

Vulcans carry the racial memory of their predecessors and with meditation can relive the events of Surak, or as far back as the first Wanderer. Each met with the intelligent being that lives in the soul of the planet. Each Vulcan is interconnected. When Spock traveled back in time, he found the lack of contact with other Vulcans led his intellect to return to the pre-Reform past. When a Vulcan dies, the bondmate must be kept in close mental contact with other family members or that individual will also die, due to psychic withdrawal. This is one reason bonded Vulcans seldom travel on separate craft or without other Vulcans in proximity.

Amanda Grayson, one of the key originators of the first universal translator, took much of the responsibility for the translation difficulty that rearranged "master" into "suppress." Grayson married Sarek, son of Skor, Vulcan ambassador to Terra. She became the first Terran to become oldest mother to the house of Surak. Sarek's second Terran wife succeeded her, but Grayson will always be remembered for carrying the katra of T'Pau, after the ancient Vulcan legend chose her to unify the planets at a time of disunity.

Vulcans trained in the mental arts are able to pass their katra into another living being and have that "life force" or "karma" transmuted into the living thoughts of the Hall of Ancient Records. In one case (Spock again), the katra was restored to a new body created by the molecular regeneration of the Genesis effect. Scientists and philosophers continue to debate the points of that event, triggered by Khan Noonian Singh, the 20th century man who altered 23rd century events after awakening from suspended animation.

Spock's rejoining of mind and body had been preserved in legends, performed at the sharp edge of illogic. Leonard H. Edward McCoy, son of David, carried the katra until the ceremony was performed on Mt. Seleya, where the Tribe of the Eye and Tribe of the mind-meld first decided to cooperate. Ancient

Vulcan considers the word "neighbor" and "enemy" indistinguishable, since each battle for finite resources separated by a common border. Romulans also carry this trait in their genetic memory, but have lost the traits of the mental-arts since they lost the secrets of emotional suppression.

VULCAN SECRETS

Vulcan physiology is dependent upon brain action. A Vulcan healing trance can cure injuries that would kill most other species. Vulcan hearing and vision is acute and they also possess great physical strength and a photographic memory. They are reluctant to touch other beings due to their telepathic nature. Vulcans' passivity is often mistaken for weakness, but they can kill and murder if it is for a logical purpose.

Vulcan mind-control techniques have been perfected over the centuries allowing Vulcans to kill with thought. Vulcans prefer large estates with stone walls and unlocked doors. Gardens of rock, flower and vegetable are tended with care, as the vegetarian population of more than 7 billion on the home planet must be sustained.

The Vulcanian Expedition was a misnamed attempt by the

Federation to force Vulcan to provide citizens to help defend and explore the quadrant. James Kirk was a junior officer who never set foot on the planet until years later when he was invited to attend Spock's marriage to T'Pring, which became transformed into a challenge and personal combat.

Vulcan agreed to build the USS Intrepid and a series of craft manned primarily by Vulcans, who then felt uncomfortable with alien species due to their past encounters with pirates in the disastrous first contact that led to the Romulan exodus.

Vulcan sent several scout ships to survey Earth and keep track of human history. Much of our history from the period before and during the Post-Atomic Horror is courtesy of Vulcan scout ships. The first contact with Terra officially came in the mid-21st century when a Vulcan scout was rescued by a United Nations vessel near the outer region of the Terran system. It is now believed that visit was arranged to allow the humans to first learn of the Centaurians before an encounter with racial aliens.

ROMULANS

Ages ago, in the days of pre-Surak Vulcan, one of the warring Vulcan tribes chose to take the chance of leaving the planet itself using the then primitive form of space flight the planet had developed. Feeling threatened when alien pirates raided Vulcan, this segment, called The Wanderers, chose to break off from pre-Reform Vulcan society completely and travel to twin worlds far away which its astronomers had discovered.

These planets were unknown to the rest of Vulcan and so the ex-Vulcans correctly determined that they would be left unhampered to follow their course of societal evolution. Due to the already experienced off-world threat, the Wanderers remained suspicious of all alien craft, considering them enemies until proven otherwise. And if the aliens did not prove to be enemies then they would be conquered to prevent them from ever becoming the enemies of the Wanderers.

These two worlds, which came to be known as Romulus and Remus in the Terran dialects, allowed the warlike Vulcan offshoot to prosper and grow. As time passed they became even more militaristic, developing a society which reflected their constant state of war. Personal liberty was controlled by the state and serving in the military was the highest goal one could attain. A celebrity in Romulan society is a war hero or the commander of a Romulan battle cruiser.

In the 22nd century a Romulan vessel encountered a Federation ship and fired on it. The Federation ship managed to defend itself and limp back to the nearest starbase. More ships were dispatched to the area where another battle ensued. When attempts to arrive at peaceful relations with the Romulans failed, the Federation declared war. The battles were fought by ships which did not have the kind of visual ship-to-ship communications technologies commonly in use a century later.

When an armistice was declared, it was done via ship to ship communications without ever meeting as the Romulans refused to have personal contact with the aliens of the Federation. A neutral zone was established which the Romulans could use with impunity, but since they refused to join the Federation and renounce their warlike ways, the Romulans were forbidden to leave that Neutral Zone.

BREAKING OUT OF THE NEUTRAL ZONE

In the 23rd century, Romulan scientists developed a cloaking device which enabled a vessel to be invisible to both visual and sensor devices. This was combined with a

new plasma weapon of previously unrecorded strength. The Romulan flagship was equipped with these devices and began a raid on the Federation outposts along the Neutral Zone.

The Enterprise managed to intercept the vessel and outsmart its captain, resulting in the destruction of the Romulan ship and their abandoning of plans to expand outside the rigid borders of the Neutral Zone. A later mission of the Enterprise had them deliberately penetrate the Neutral Zone and steal a cloaking device from a Romulan vessel, thus creating a parity of technology between the two sides.

By the end of the 23rd century the Romulans had completely withdrawn beyond their borders and refused any sort of commerce with the worlds outside. In the 24th century, after an absence of 50 years, the Romulans once more made themselves known to the Federation.

They still refused to join the Federation and retained the position of an armed truce as before. There have been some skirmishes between Romulan and Federation ships, but no overt acts of war. An attempt by the Romulans to capture the Enterprise-D inside the Neutral Zone was thwarted by the intervention of the Federation's now staunch allies The Klingons.

On the other hand, when a Romulan ship suffered core damage and was in danger of self-destructing, the Enterprise-D offered to assist in the rescue effort and thereby saved the entire crew of the Romulan vessel.

These now distant cousins of Vulcans, the war-like Romulans, have remained constant as enemies of the Federation in both centuries. However there is a ray of hope. Many Romulans who are tired of war have formed an underground organization whose object is to effect a peace treaty and become respected and peaceful members of the galaxy. In this they have help from an unexpected quarter. Mr. Spock, former Starfleet Officer and current Federation ambassador, is secretly working with the Romulan underground. His wish is to not only end the hostilities, but by the arrival of the 25th century, to see the Romulans united with their distant relatives on Vulcan.

THE KLINGONS

The Klingon culture is a rich and vibrant one that continues to evolve as the finer traditions of valor and honor overcome millennia of civil war. Previously, wars of con-

quest had led to the brutal first contact with the ch'Rhiani and Terrans in which they frightened their enemies into decades of bloodshed.

Klingon culture is best exemplified by its language. Although the peoples of the Empire each share a root tongue, there are literally thousands of variations in the provinces that make up the greater Klingon Empire as it now exists following the Organian Treaties and Federation Alliance Agreement.

For example, in the simple statement "I have, my lord," a Klingon operative named Valkris was able to convey several meanings per sentence. She was giving her lover permission to destroy the ship she was on, yet receiving a great gift in that Kruge would help restore her family name, and for this she would gladly forfeit her existence.

In that four word message, Valkris conveyed permission in the second stratum and forgiveness in the third. Ironically, Kruge was killed by (then) Admiral James T. Kirk and never was able to complete his promise. Kruge was eulogized as a great warrior and many years later another Enterprise captain would travel aboard a ship named Kruge to Romulus to meet Kirk's former First Officer.

Another example of Klingon psychology involves the tale of a great warrior called before the Emperor to destroy the other family in power to help him consolidate his own power. The operative was completely successful in his mission, after he was able to get information from a friend of his father.

However, as a payment for the information, he agreed to assassinate an officer that stood in the way of the supplier's son. He was expected to be honored for his great success, yet instead, found out he was to be executed for that favor he had done. It turned out that the friend's father wanted an unknown, illegitimate grandson of the Emperor out of the way. The operative actually savored the irony of the trap, that he was used skillfully by the man who managed to save his son's life at no familial obligation.

The irony becomes deeper when it becomes known that operative's accomplice was none other than (the then) Second Officer Kruge, who became Captain upon the death of his superiors after Spock and a young boy named David Marcus (Kirk's son) set the traps that entangled Kruge's superiors. The man who died at the Emperor's hand was given a chance for honorable death. The Emperor understood, yet could not let it be known that he had failed to avenge the grandson.

THE RETURN OF A LEGEND

For the first time in three centuries a Klingon emperor has arisen—none other than the legendary warrior Kahless himself!

In the 24th century, when Worf visited Borath, a holy planet, he encountered a Klingon being who purported to be the returning founder of Klingon culture. Worf was the "doubting Thomas" of the Klingon disciples, yet a DNA scan convinced him of the being's claim. When Gawron, leader of the High Council, bested Kahless in battle with knives, Worf confronted Koroth, leader of the Klingon Elders of Boroth. He admitted that the return of Kahless was made possible through cloning and memory augmentation. This allowed the elders to construct a clone with the memories of the Klingon Founder.

Worf realized that he could help restore the Empire's moral decay and worked an agreement that allowed Kahless to ascend to the Emperor's throne as the "rightful heir" to Kahless' legacy. This compromise saved the Empire from civil war. It was the second Klingon conflict that Worf involved himself in, the first being when he convinced his brother Kurn to support Gawron over Duras's family in the previous skirmish. Worf had his honor restored and his good family name was returned to him and Kurn.

Kurn now serves on the High Council. Duras died on his own ship after Worf defeated him with his Batlah (Sword of Honor) in retaliation for the death of Worf's mate K'ehylr, who was killed by Duras after he found out she knew of his father's betrayal of the Klingons to the Romulans at the Khitomer Massacre. She was half-Klingon and is the mother of Worf's son Alexander. Worf received a formal reprimand for the ritual assassination of his mate's killer.

Worf's diplomacy (an oxymoron, some might say) in showing Federation officers that a Klingon can work effectively with them has been immeasurable in helping to bring down the barriers between the two cultures. Klingon self-defense classes have become popular in the Federation. Many Terrans speak Klingonese with most high-caste Klingons speaking Galactic Standard, although universal translators help prevent misunderstandings.

A HISTORY OF HATRED

The first contact between the two cultures led to centuries of war because neither understood the other's psychology. Much of current first-contact procedure was designed to prevent such occurrences in which two ships miscommunicate and millions die as a result. The Romulan and Klingon first contacts rank among the deadliest in Terran and Federation history with the deaths in the first year of any of the wars equal to all the inter-human wars, nuclear and conventional, in the entire history of humanity as a species. Billions died and trillions suffered in 22nd, 23rd and 24th century Federation annals.

For all of his professional career, James Kirk fought, distrusted and hated Klingons, and the feeling was mutual. The Klingon high command had early-on put a price on Kirk's head and promised great rewards to any captain who captured the coveted Enterprise, along with its captain.

When Kirk's son, Dr. David Marcus, was murdered at the Genesis planet on the orders of Klingon Commander Kruge, Kirk's hate knew no bounds. Yet despite these emotional feelings, he and his crew were instrumental in preventing the disruption of the peace treaty at Khitomer which would lead to the end of the devastating wars.

Thus the enemies of the 23rd century are the friends of the 24th (with a few notable exceptions who find their careers as warriors threatened). Although no humans are known to be serving on Klingon ships as yet on a regular basis, one Klingon, the very efficient Lieutenant Worf, is security officer of the once hated Enterprise.

THE BAJORA

Bajora was a thriving world of artists, philosophers and other craftsmen at a time when Earth was still uncivilized. Their proud history suffered when the Cardassian Empire claimed the planet and began a multi-decade control that brought about millions of deaths before the Cardassians decided to cut their losses and end the occupation.

Bajorans fled their homeworld and were often abused by the people they encountered, due to a series of lies and misperceptions that became acceptable as many other stereotyped groups can attest to. Bajor recently gained full independence and is considering applying for membership in the Federation. Bajor requested Federation assistance in the maintaining of an abandoned Cardassian mining station and it proved beneficial when the Federation officers discovered the first known stable wormhole. These resulted in the opening up of trade with the Gamma Quadrant, making Bajor a key weigh station that increases their wealth at a time when Bajor desperately needs to recover from the years of brutal rule by the Cardassian overseers.

THE BORG

The Borg culture consists of an all-consuming uni-mind that strangles the individuality of the persons that the connected units absorb into the collective. For this reason the Borg are the most dangerous race yet encountered. They learn from every encounter and never make the same mistake twice. Their strength allows the Borg to literally think action. Their only known weakness involves the ability to enter their uni-mind by direct contact.

The extreme danger makes it unlikely that any attempt to unite with the Borg will take place any time soon. The Borg destroyed the home planet of the legendary race of listeners who were spread throughout the galaxy in an attempt to preserve their race. A member of this race was on board the USS Enterprise when it first encountered the race at J-27.

The Q entity had transported the starship there to show what perils humanity faced as it continues to explore the galaxy. The Enterprise lost 18 lives in the initial encounter. The Borg later attempted a direct attack on Earth, where the beings destroyed an armada of starships at Wolf 359, commanded by Admiral Hansen. The Borg had absorbed Enterprise Captain Jean-Luc Picard and used his knowledge to overcome Federation defense strategy.

After the Enterprise attacked the Borg ship and retrieved "Locutus," the being created from Picard's mind and body, they were able to use the connection with the Borg to place a self-destruct sequence into their programming by requiring them to return to sleep mode during the Terran attack. Contact was made seconds before the Enterprise would have rammed the Borg ship at warp speed in a last ditch attempt to save the blue ball of humanity from assimilation.

The Borg remain the most mysterious and unapproachable race which the Federation have encounter as they believe only in assimilation, not communication or any other form of peaceful relations. The origin of the Borg, and how they went from a humanoid race to one which became a hive mind with mechanical extensions attached from the moment of birth, is unknown.

CENTAURIONS

The residents of Athens (Centaurus) were the first intelligent beings Terrans found when they began to explore the galaxy. The first contact occurred in the mid-21st century, when the United Nations vessel, The Icarus, traveled to the closest star system to Sol, only four light years away. Alpha Centauri-A is a yellow sun, slightly larger and brighter than Sol. Centauri-A is surrounded by fifteen planets, of which only Centaurus contains life. The inner planets are terrestrial rock and the outer planets are gas giants (like the Terran solar system).

The second star in the three star system, is Alpha Centauri-B. It was 30 A.U.s from A. (An A.U. is the length of light from the Earth to Sol.) Centauri-B suffered a massive expansion in a rare time displacement and grew into an orange, then red, giant. All of the six planets in orbit of B had been named after characters in Terra's SUPERMAN comic books. Kent was the largest colony. Tens of millions were safely evacuated, although 184 stayed behind for the immolation of the planet.

The inner planet, Olsen, was consumed, followed by Perry, Lang,

Kent, Lane and Luthor. All were destroyed and the outer gas giants of Centaurus-A were singed, but increased shielding saved Athens, the Centauri homeworld. Proxima Centauri, the third star in the system, is a red dwarf that is perhaps best known for being the closer star to Sol.

A popular tourist attraction on Centaurus is land owned by Capt. James T. Kirk. Kirk named his land Garrovick Valley, after his late former captain. The river dividing the land is named the Farragut River after the ship Kirk served aboard during the Farragut disaster. The former Chief Medical Officer on the Enterprise, Leonard H. Edward McCoy, is a legal resident of Centaurus and holds Centauri citizenship, although he is originally from the region of the southern United States known as Georgia.

THE HAND OF THE PRESERVERS

Centaurans are believed to have been brought from Terra by an ancient race known as the "Preservers," who took humans from Earth during the rise of Greek civilization. They refer to their homeworld as Athens. Zefrem Cochrane, the inventor of the warp drive principle, is perhaps the most famous Centauran. They are genetically identical to humans, with one exception. They have an extra joint in one finger, that can be noticed during a handshake. The Centaurans welcomed the arrival of the Icarus and Cochrane traveled to Earth before disappearing years later.

A recently declassified log indicates the Enterprise had an encounter with a claimant purporting to be Cochrane, but details are sketchy. The reason Earth observers had not noticed the technological activity can be attributed to the fact that a form of xenophobia was fostered to a Centauran king. He had made defense a priority and massive shielding devices protected the environment from pollution, electromagnetic pulse waves and other methods that modern industrial societies display. If the Icarus had not been specifically sent to the closest planet, it is likely that sensors would have failed to pick up any sign of life.

In effect, the Centaurans developed a Romulan-like fear of endangering their planet, yet for far different reasons. It is believed that Terra's space program was enhanced by first making contact with a similar culture, as first contact with more "alien" life forms might have led to a planetwide wave of xenophobia.

TELLARITES AND ANDORIANS

These two races are well known in both the 23rd and 24th centuries. The passage of time has changed them little. The Tellarites are loud, boisterous and love a good argument. This is an innate part of their culture, and is one of their main forms of entertainment, and they aren't likely to change. They are valued members of the Federation, and their instinctive knowledge of engineering sciences has contributed greatly to ship-building technology.

Tellarites value an outward display of arrogance so highly that even their ambassadors practice it. They feel that restraint is a sign of weakness and resent the fact that Vulcans not only believe and practice the opposite but look down on Tellarites as being primitive and undisciplined. While Vulcans tolerate Tellarites, Tellarites hate Vulcans as they believe that the Vulcan people regard Tellarites as savages since the people of the time of pre-Reform Vulcan acted very much like the way Tellarites do now. Since Tellarites know that Vulcans believe in hiding their emotions they constantly look for opportunities to goad the Vulcans they meet in the hope of piercing that well practiced unemotional facade.

Although they place great value on family and their offspring, the Andorians are a violent race. They will not pick an argument, but once provoked, their brutal fighting ability is the envy of even the Klingons. Fortunately they are also members of the Federation, and not a race that will attack a ship just because it gets in their way.

Because of their value on family, Andorians reproduce prolifically. An androgynous race, they possess both male and female sexual characteristics. They are neutral except at periods of mating when one of the sexual characteristics will predominate. The Andorian populations on their homeworlds have increased at such a high rate that they have been seeking to peacefully expand onto other worlds. But because other worlds regard the Andorians as practicing overpopulation without responsible self-restraint, not all worlds welcome Andorian colonization.

ALIENS KNOWN AND UNKNOWN

So why are some species who played major roles in one century, not known in the other? There is no clear answer to this question, but the most frequently voiced opinion/theory is that Kirk's Enterprise traveled and explored in a different part of the galaxy than the newest flagship under Picard's leadership. This is a very real probability since the Federation has only explored eleven percent of the galaxy.

This would explain why each century has its own demons and angels. This explains why Kirk never made contact with the greedy Ferengi or the deceitful Cardassians, and why Picard escaped having to contend with the Capellans or Talosians.

Each captain has been forced into alien hand-to-hand combat—Picard with the invisible electro-magnetic entity he encountered while trying to communicate with the Children of Tama, and Kirk with the reptilian Gorn.

Wouldn't Kirk have loved to have had a Betazoid telepath to tell him what an adversary was planning? Picard certainly wouldn't object if a group of Organians happened along in time to put a stop to a Borg attack.

Lest we forget, Kirk had tribbles and Picard had nanites.

When chroniclers of the 25th century compare the good and the bad of the two previous centuries, they will likely find that the names of the species and worlds may differ, but that the good and evil encountered will balance each other out.

When "Q" claimed to be god, just how much was he exaggerating?

In the NEXT GENERATION episode "Tapestry," Jean-Luc Picard suffers a life-threatening injury and lies near death on the operating table as Dr. Crusher and her medical team struggle to revive him. Picard, however, finds himself in a glowing white landscape, a classic near-death experience marred by one glaring exception: Q is there, greeting Picard as benevolently as he can, with two startling pieces of bad news: "You're dead and I'm god."

Chapter Seven
THE "Q" QUESTION

In the ensuing storyline, Q allows Picard to relive a crucial incident in his youth that led to his need for an artificial heart. Picard is again confronted with the question of whether or not he should help his friend Corey rig a gambling game in order to get back at some Nausiccan rowdies; his unresolved relationship with the woman Marta also faces him once more.

But doing the right thing in regards to Corey only leads to further complications, and sleeping with Marta— which he did not do in real life— only adds more bitterness to this relationship with one of the earliest women Picard left behind.

And his life after this does not proceed well, either. This, obviously, was the turning point which led the young, brash Jean-Luc Picard to rethink his life and change it, leading to his development into a thoughtful leader of men. The "new" Picard created in this Q scenario is not the same man we all know and admire. Of course, Picard is returned back to his life as he (and we) know it when Crusher finally manages to save him; as in "Inner Light," the subjective events have taken place in a relatively short amount of objective time. But all of this raises an intriguing question: who, and what, exactly, is Q, anyway?

In this episode, Q tells Picard that he is god. Could this be true? It's well worth looking into. At the very least— could the entities of the "Q" continuum be gods of some sort? Whatever they are, they are obviously more highly evolved than humans. We could probably never answer the question of their divinity adequately, and it seems likely that, in a universe created by Gene Roddenberry, they probably wouldn't be gods in any supernatural sense, but would fit into some evolutionary niche above mere mortals. But what is their real relationship with humans? And does the Q portrayed by John deLancie represent them as well as he could?

EVOLVING "Q"

When we first encountered Q in "Encounter At Farpoint," he seemed to be a self-appointed judge of humanity, and more than a bit similar to the alien child Trelane whom James T. Kirk encountered on the classic STAR TREK episode "Squire of Gothos." But while Trelane was revealed to be nothing more than the spoiled brat of super-

evolved aliens, Q seemed to have no such Achilles' heel.

In his second outing, "Hide And Q," he again tested the Enterprise crew. In "Q Who" he really threw a wrench into the works by introducing humanity and its allied species to the Borg. In "Deja Q" he was stripped of his powers by his own unseen compatriots (represented briefly on-screen by Corbin Bernson of L.A. LAW fame) for going too far in his dealings with humans.

"Q-Pid" had him transplanting the Enterprise crew into a Robin Hood scenario, and, shortly before "Tapestry," he appeared to menace a young Enterprise intern who turns out to be a Q as well, in "True Q." All of these outings revealed different aspects of Q and his fellow omnipotent entities, but they still add up to little more than clues. Who is he, really?

To begin with, it is uncertain that Q's motives are always in line with those of his Continuum. Usually, he appears to interfere with humans, in a maliciously malevolent fashion. He seems to regard these meddlesome excursions as a mission of some sort— do the Q, as a collective, see it as their mission to test evolving life forms by presenting them with conundrums, paradoxes and challenges? No matter how obnoxious the manner of Q might be, his antics invariably do point up some aspect of human behavior, even when the story is played merely for laughs.

It would seem evident, from the events presented in "Deja Q," that his actions don't generally conflict with those of his peers, just that his methods sometimes earn their disapproval. Even though the other Q glimpsed in that episode seems to be just about as seedy an individual as John deLancie's character, might it not be entirely possible that the general goal of the Q Continuum is a benevolent one? Where the Federation has the hands-off policy embodied in the Prime Directive (leave other folks alone to develop in their own way), the Q might very well take a different approach to "inferior" species, goading them towards further evolutionary advances. On the other hand, it would seem apparent that the Q are amoral in any human sense, not above using moral terminology in their attacks on humans though processes (as in the trial in "Encounter At Farpoint") but generally in the position of viewing all moral beliefs as relative and arbitrary.

THE NATURE OF Q-NESS

Case in point: the still mysterious fate of Guinan's race. When Guinan and Q encountered each other in "Q Who," it was revealed that the two characters had met before— and that Q was actually intimidated by Guinan! When the Borg came into the picture, Guinan revealed that it was, in fact, the Borg who destroyed most of her race and their home world. She did not reveal whether or not Q had been responsible for unleashing the Borg on her people, but he (or one of his fellow Q) could very well have done so. Perhaps the Q have chosen the Borg on other occasions, as a test of some race's mettle. Of course, it would also seem that this particular scheme of Q's aroused the ire of his own kind, leading them to cast him, naked and powerless, on the Enterprise bridge.

And here we discovered that Q had real reason to fear Guinan, whose previous experience with this trickster led her to the imminently practical test of stabbing him with a fork to see if his latest visit was not just another ruse. It was not— but could this entire scenario have been part of a larger scheme by the Q Continuum? We have no way of knowing whether or not the Q Continuum acts in any sort of concerted effort, or if each individual Q is a relatively free agent of sorts.

Of course, in "True Q," Q appears, quite specifically, as an agent of his Continuum, sent to test Amanda and to present her with an ultimatum: join the Q and embrace your powers, or live as a human and renounce them utterly, the only third alternative being death. (And since Amanda's parents, "retired" Q living on Earth, were killed by the forces of the Continuum, it would seem that Q can be killed— although, perhaps, only by another Q.) And again, once Amanda chooses humanity, Q tests her until she succumbs to the temptation to use her power, and must admit that she is a Q.

Tempting and testing seem to be the things that Q is best at, with taunting making a third and final "T" in the equation. He has much in common with the tricksters who abound in world folklore. But most of all, he truly resembles that most famous trickster of them all, the Devil. The question of Q's divinity, as claimed in "Tapestry," is not completely undermined by this; one must remember that Satan, a.k.a. Lucifer, was a fallen angel, once a most trusted servant of God. And in the Book of Job a most unusual view of Satan is presented: he is seen almost to still be working for God, despite the widely publicized labor dispute so exhaustively portrayed by John Milton in PARADISE LOST.

And Satan's job seems to be specifically the testing of humans and their character. And in earlier religious traditions, there can frequently be found (usually in that troublesome life-after-death phase) a figure who acts sort of as an attorney for the prosecution, while another prototypical Jesus figure acts as defense, weighing the worth of the human soul in question. Q can be seen as a reflection of this aspect of myth.

Later refinements of the Satan legend, most notably the Fausts of Christopher Marlowe and Johann Goethe, depict the devil as both a bringer of knowledge and of difficult decisions. In short, a figure who makes humans think, and question both themselves and their beliefs. Q fits right in here. Although humans like Picard and Riker obstinately resist his tests and temptations, he is so superciliously smug because he knows that things really aren't the way they believe them to be!

Q-TIPS

While THE NEXT GENERATION often uses Q just for laughs, or for setting up a cute scenario like the Robin Hood plotline of "Q-Pid," it is obvious that Q is a character of great unplumbed depths. Fortunately, his two most recent outings on THE NEXT GENERATION, "True Q" and "Tapestry," have used him to true dramatic effect. (Although the same cannot be said of his sole appearance to date on STAR TREK—DEEP SPACE NINE, it seems pointless to waste John deLancie's fine comedic talents by making a grim Satanic figure out of Q!) Q's claim that he is god certainly raises an interesting question. In angelic literature, God does not speak directly, but through an angel called Metatron, this angel literally being the "Voice Of God."

God, being ineffable, uses the angels as his physical (or semi-physical) representatives— an idea used by Milton, influenced by the Kabalah. Some radical mystical views even see the devil as a fallen aspect of God, God being incomplete without him. So how can we say that there is absolutely no validity to Q's claim? Of course, omnipotent fellow that he appears to be, Q would certainly have no problem popping into Picard's mind at the crucial moment in "Tapestry," there to quite literally mess with the good Captain's head while it was most vulnerable.

But what, ultimately, was the point of Q's meddling here? Basically, the entire upshot is that Picard accepts that his life is, of necessity, best the way it has already turned out. If anything, Q's interference has helped Picard rid himself of any of the regrets he may have retained from that earlier part of his life, a change that can only strengthen Picard's character. If this was really Q, and not merely some projection of Picard's brain in the face of death, one cannot help but wonder if this was not really a positive experience for Picard. Could Q really be the agent of some higher power?

Since this is Gene Roddenberry's STAR TREK universe, it seems unlikely that the entities of the Q Continuum are some sort of pre-existing, supernatural realm. They're probably just another alien race at a farther stage of evolution who have a troublesome tendency to give other races the occasional swift kick in the backside.

As in the case of the Borg, the Q are willing to risk destroying other races in the pursuit of their mysterious agenda. But are their motives ultimately benevolent, if extreme? Perhaps they just use the Borg as a means of assuring some sort of cosmic Darwinian scheme, weeding out the weak and promulgating the survival of the fittest? Or are they simply evil plotters who enjoy mischief? Clearly, the destruction of entire races can't be their real agenda, since they obviously have the power to destroy anything they choose to— or are they restrained, not by their own will, but by some other power? Odds are we will never know for sure. But one thing, at least, is certain— we can never take Q for granted. Whenever he shows up, things are bound to heat up, hellishly or otherwise.

The Captain. The First Officer. The Science Officer. These are the personnel of the starship Enterprise, both yesterday and today.

It is often true that the first person to embark on a particular endeavor will set the standards for those who follow. Now it is true that James T. Kirk was not the initial commander of the starship Enterprise—that honor went first to Robert April, and later to Christopher Pike. But the general consensus is that it was Kirk who set the standards for future generations.

Impossible standards, many who followed him thought, but not for Jean-Luc Picard, a man who came along nearly a century later. Picard would set a few standards of his own.

Both Kirk and Picard would figure prominently in the record books and historical chronicles of Starfleet. But how do they compare to each other? How do their styles of command differ? How are they similar?

Chapter
Eight
THE PRIMARY BRIDGE CREWS OF THE ENTERPRISE

What kind of private lives did they lead? How were they perceived by their crews and senior officers? Were these feelings returned? Did they consider themselves warriors or explorers? And perhaps most important, how did the Prime Directive affect their command decisions?

Both men were born into agricultural families—Kirk on a farm in Iowa, Picard on a grape vineyard in France—but neither had the least desire to embrace the family business as a career. Each had an older brother with whom they frequently clashed, and each had a mother they dearly loved. Perhaps the one quality they both possessed was an abundant love of adventure.

BY KAY DOTY

KIRK—IN THE BEGINNING

James T. Kirk, whose father George was a Starfleet officer before him, always had his eyes turned to the stars. He became the youngest cadet to enter Starfleet Academy when he was accepted prior to his seventeenth birthday. He was also the youngest to graduate, and the youngest to become a starship Captain. He would later be one of the youngest to become an admiral.

The darling of his teachers, Kirk studied hard and always had his assignments in on time. Many years later he admitted that he had been,

STAR TREK cast at MANN's CHINESE THEATRE on December 5, 1991.

Photo by Chris Flicker

". . . pretty grim. . . " during his Academy days.

Although he occasionally went out with friends, and was even involved in a fracas or two, his chief source of irritation was an upper classman named Finnegan who seemed to have made it his mission to make life miserable for Kirk.

Upon graduation, Kirk worked hard and moved rapidly up through the ranks and duty on smaller ships. He was serving on the USS Farragut during the battle with pirates from Epsilon-Canaris III when he was badly injured but stayed at his post until the battle ended. He was taken, along with nearly half of the crew, to the nearest Starbase where they were treated for their injuries. Kirk's leg was shattered, but the base physician, Lieutenant Leonard McCoy, repaired the damage.

Thanks to McCoy's expertise, Kirk's career was saved and he returned to duty. His promotion to Captain and assignment to command of the USS Enterprise NCC-1701 was due in part to the commendations and recommendations of his Farragut commander, Captain Garrovick. Kirk repaid McCoy for his efforts in saving his leg by naming him Chief Medical Officer of the Enterprise—one of his first assignments.

THE ENTERPRISE AND COMPANY

The appointment to command the Enterprise did not come without a few strings—Kirk inherited many of Captain Pike's crew. One of these was Commander Spock, the Vulcan who served as Pike's science officer. When Kirk was given the Enterprise, he was also given an order to retain the Vulcan—in the dual capacity of science and first officer.

Commander Gary Mitchell, Kirk's buddy from their Academy days, was his choice as second in command, but Starfleet said no. They did allow Mitchell to serve as Kirk's navigator, although Mitchell died in the line of duty early in Kirk's first five-year mission.

This was Kirk's first experience with the death of a crewman under his command, and it was particularly difficult because the pair had been close friends since their cadet days. In addition, Kirk felt guilty over Gary's death, wrongly believing that he could have somehow prevented it had he taken a different action.

Gradually Kirk began to depend more and more on the quiet, knowledgeable Vulcan and soon began to consider him and McCoy as his two closest friends.

But he didn't exclude his other senior officers, frequently inviting them to spend shore leave with him. After he began his duties at the Admiralty, and on the rare occasions when duty brought the Enterprise back to Earth, Kirk entertained his former crew in his home. He always felt a loss when they returned to the Enterprise, leaving him behind.

THE GALACTIC LOTHARIO

It was said by those who knew him best that Kirk was "married" to the Enterprise, as many of the best ship captains are. But while he shunned the more conventional form of marriage, this captain certainly did not shun members of the feminine gender.

Known by some as the galactic Lothario, he did leave a few broken hearts in his wake, but also suffered his share of fractures in that region as well. The encounter that left him with unending pain was his love affair with Carol Marcus that resulted in the birth of their son, David Marcus. When David was murdered by the Klingon Kruge on the Genesis Planet, not only did a part of himself die, but Kirk developed an undying hatred of everything Klingon.

Kirk had a flamboyant style of command. He always wanted to be in the midst of the action, and once admitted that he inclined to, " . . . go where angels fear to tread." He led most landing parties, frequently placing his own life in peril.

When Starfleet Command decreed that ship's captains could better serve both the fleet and the Federation, as well as the landing party, by remaining aboard ship, Kirk was devastated. He hated the inaction, but even more he hated to delegate others to serve on dangerous missions when he couldn't share that danger. He did, on occasions when the ship was in the far reaches of the galaxy, disobey that dictate. When he did so, he reasoned that he was the only one who could successfully deal with the situation at hand.

In this there were times when he was probably right, for Kirk had earned his galaxy-wide reputation as a warrior, a diplomat, and an honest man who kept his word. There were many worlds that feared him, and had even put a price on his head, naming him the number one enemy of their world—usually because he had defeated them at their own nefarious game.

THE ULTIMATE IN LOYALTY

His engaging personality and ready smile, his willingness to defend his crew, and to share all dangers with them, earned him their complete loyalty. This was proven, not only when he resumed command of the Enterprise during the Probe crisis, but later when he stole the Enterprise to rescue Spock.

After the rescue, the crew all went into exile on Vulcan with him, accompanying him back to Earth when Kirk was ordered to return and face Court Martial. This included Commander Sulu who placed his chance to command the Excelsior in jeopardy, to remain at his Captain's side. And again, they were there to support him when he was ordered to bring his old enemy, the hated Klingons, to Earth for a peace conference.

This same crew again risked court martial when they ignored orders to return to Federation Headquarters. Instead they worked frantically to rescue Kirk and McCoy, both of whom had been captured, tried and convicted of the murder of Chancellor Gorkon. Also on hand was Sulu, now Captain of the Excelsior who again put his command at risk to assist Kirk and his former shipmates. In the process, they exposed those who were actually responsible for the murder.

Unable to think of returning to command headquarters to go into retirement, to part with this crew, Kirk ordered a course heading to the, "Second star to the right and straight on until morning."

JEAN-LUC PICARD

Picard knew from his earliest boyhood that he had no desire to spend his entire life in the company of grapes. But unlike Kirk, his eyes weren't always on the stars.

Becoming an archaeologist was the dream of Picard's youth, and he was happiest when digging in the bowels of the Earth, searching for a sign or some evidence of an ancient civilization. However, as his studies in his chosen field progressed, he began to realize there was far more to learn about the long-forgotten past out in space than there was on Earth, and he began to toy with the idea of space exploration.

Over the objections of his archeology professors, Picard applied for admittance to Starfleet Academy, and was rejected. Deeply disappointed, he returned home and began an intensive course of study. The following year he was accepted.

The young cadet's career almost ended during his senior year when he and two classmates were spending the night on the town. A brawl ensued and Picard was stabbed in the heart. That could have been the end of not only his career, but his life, had not his quick-thinking friends rushed him to the Academy sickbay. The damage was too severe to be repaired, so doctors replaced his own heart with a cardiac unit.

After the brush with disaster, a more subdued Picard graduated with honors, although not as the first in his class. During his years as an under classman the temptation to enjoy the local night life with his friends had prevented him from giving his studies quite the attention he should have.

AN AMAZING STARFLEET CAREER

Picard served on two small vessels, compiling an exemplary work record, thus proving the wildness of his youth had been removed along with his heart. This record and his continuing interest in archeology earned him the command of the science vessel, the USS Stargazer while still in his thirties.

Picard commanded the Stargazer on an amazing 22-year mission. During the course of the mission his explorations and discoveries made him a legend in his own time. This growing reputation would later earn him the command of the newly commissioned USS Enterprise NCC-1701-D.

The Stargazer captain loved his command, but when he said goodbye he carried the sadness of two great losses. The first was the death of his good friend Commander Jack Crusher.

Crusher was killed while in command of an Away Team, and Picard, like Kirk with Gary Mitchell, always blamed himself for Jack's death because he had been the one to send him on the mission. Picard took his friend's body back to Earth where he met Jack's wife, Dr. Beverly Crusher, and their young son, Wesley.

The second was the loss of the Stargazer itself in a battle with one of Starfleet's first encounters with the Ferengi. Attacked for no apparent reason, the ship was disabled. Picard ordered the crew to abandon ship and they drifted in a shuttlecraft for over two months before being rescued. Much later Picard learned that their attackers wanted the Stargazer for the price it would bring. He never stopped blaming himself for the loss of his ship.

THE BURDENS OF COMMAND

After learning he had been given his secret dream to command Starfleet's flagship, Picard discovered that Beverly Crusher had requested assignment to the Enterprise as Chief Medical Officer.

With remnants of guilt over her husband's death still in his mind, he suggested that she might be happier on another ship. But she insisted and eventually he accepted her and would be glad that he did. He wasn't prepared for her teenaged genius son, Wesley.

The new Enterprise captain did not agree with Starfleet Command's decision to allow families of the crew to live aboard ship. As a man who had no children of his own, he was uncomfortable around them, suspected that he didn't like them and fervently wished they were on another ship—any ship but the Enterprise!

Picard had the privilege of selecting his own crew, and with his 25 years of experience as a Starfleet officer to call upon, he knew the records of most of the applicants. Consequently he assembled a skilled crew who could work together like a well oiled machine.

THE COMMAND CREW

He respects, and is genuinely fond of all of his senior officers, and is congenial in one-on-one chats, be it personal or professional. Picard is inclined to be a loner and doesn't include crew members on his shore leaves.

Except for an occasional concert, reception or fencing match, there is little socializing between captain and crew. If Picard ever sits in on their jazz sessions or weekly poker games, the crew has never mentioned it, although he would certainly be welcomed if he were to express an interest.

The crew in turn respect him and his ability to command. They obey his orders without question, like him and are one hundred and ten percent loyal. They willingly go the extra light year for him.

On the bridge, Picard is always the picture of complete control. The ship may be minutes from destruction, and the captain experiencing his own internal earthquake, but his outward demeanor is one of total confidence.

A LADY NAMED THE ENTERPRISE

When Picard first came aboard the Enterprise he referred to the gleaming, beautiful ship as "she," not an uncommon thought as ships are usually referred to in that manner. But this time his mind took him back to another "she," a woman named Celeste, whom he had loved, and who had died while he still commanded the Stargazer. After the pain of losing her had subsided, he vowed to never become romantically involved again.

Picard has engaged in an occasional romantic encounter, most notably with the irrepressible Vash, but her lifestyle is beyond his ability to tolerate, or even understand. She, in turn, could never play the dignified role of a starship captain's wife, so they went their separate ways—she with Q and he with his most demanding mistress, the Enterprise. Picard is very similar to James T. Kirk in this respect.

As we have seen, there are many differences between the two captains, but in some ways they are very much the same. Both have a deep love of books even though books have been passé for centuries. They share an active interest in history. They enjoy active sports. Picard fences and rides horses, Kirk likes to sail or go camping. They are dynamic men who live for adventure.

The most important law or order in their lives is the Prime Directive. Both men honor and respect the Directive. They understand its importance in maintaining the order of the Universe. However, both captains are aware that the people at Starfleet Command and Federation headquarters do not always understand that there are situations in which it is impossible to maintain the letter of the law. Kirk and Picard are independent thinkers, and they know that in the far reaches of the galaxy they have to do what is best, not only for their crews, their ship and themselves, but for the alien beings they encounter.

But they also have something else in common regarding the Prime Directive. They have each violated it on several occasions. But when they have, it has not been without great deliberation and only when lives were balanced in the decision. These two men bear heavily the burden of all the lives at their command.

THE FIRST OFFICERS

A ship's first officer has many more responsibilities than just filling the captain's chair when he is off the bridge and/or the ship. He is also responsible for implementing the captain's orders—to maintain a ship in perfect operating condition.

It is the first officer's duty to oversee personnel, interview newly assigned crew members and field any complaints or problems they may have. He is also responsible for the ship's smooth operation and reports any problems, either real or potential, to the Captain. But above all else the first officer is sworn to protect his captain's life, even at the cost of his own.

The captain is the final authority and may change or over-rule his second in command's order if he feels the action is justified. However he seldom does this as it could effectively undermine the first officer's ability to function in relation to the crew.

For over a century, Away Team missions have been the province of the first officer. He may either command the team himself or assign another qualified officer. This is seldom the captain. Kirk did not like that directive and a century later Picard likes it no better.

NUMBER ONE

Spock probably had less success in leading a landing party while Kirk remained on the ship than does Riker. The practice of going himself was too ingrained in Kirk for him to sit idle on the bridge while others were enjoying the adventures he craved.

Picard would also prefer to command the Away Team, after all he frequently did while commanding the Stargazer, but he didn't have William Riker as his first officer then. Picard knows that Riker is only doing his job, if a bit too arduous at times, but respects his judgment and concern,

If Picard does on occasion over-rule his Number One and something goes wrong, Picard knows that Riker will find a subtle way to indicate, ". . . I told you not to go."

The first officer must also be prepared to assume command, sometimes with only a moment's notice should the captain become ill, die or be otherwise incapacitated. The duty he probably hates the most is having to relieve his captain of duty if, in his own judgment, the captain has become unfit to command.

Usually, before taking such a step he will consult with the ship's doctor, counselor, and other senior officers. Both Spock and Riker have had to take such action, and both agonized over the decision. Later events proved their actions were the correct ones.

FIRST OFFICERS WITH A FUTURE

So how do Commander Spock and Commander Riker compare in the performance of their duty as the two best known first officers in Starfleet? Each had previously served with distinction in other capacities before becoming the second in command of Starfleet's flagship.

Soon after his graduation from Starfleet Academy, Spock was selected as the science officer by Captain Christopher Pike, commander of the Enterprise. He served in that capacity for eleven years, until Pike left the Enterprise after his promotion to fleet captain. The new commander, Captain James Kirk, not only retained him as his science officer but also as his first officer. His entire Starfleet career was spent on the Enterprise.

William Riker graduated from Starfleet Academy in just under three years, and to date has served on three ships prior to service on the Enterprise. He was first assigned to the Potemkin as a Lieutenant. He moved quickly through the chain of command and was later assigned to the USS Yorktown as second officer. From there he moved on to become first officer on the USS Hood, under Captain Jonathan DeSoto.

When Riker learned that the Enterprise NCC 1701-D had been commissioned and that the illustrious Captain Picard would be the ship's commander, Riker applied for the position of First Officer. Some thought he was making a lateral move, and that he should remain on the Hood until he was tapped for his own command, but Riker didn't see it that way. He believed that serving on the fleet's biggest and newest starship would be a healthy boost to his career.

Riker makes no secret that he wants his own command, and he has indeed been offered the center seat on three occasions, but he doesn't want just any ship. He wants the Enterprise and is willing to wait until Picard at last accepts the promotion to Admiral that he, too, has rejected three times.

STARFLEET'S BRIGHTEST LIGHTS

During the confrontation with the Borg, when Picard was captured and thought lost forever, Riker did become the Enterprise commander. After Riker instigated a daring rescue of Picard, and upon the captain's recovery, Riker relinquished the center seat and returned to his former position as second in command.

Spock, on the other hand, never wanted his own command. He did accept the captaincy of the Enterprise while his old ship was functioning as a trainer for Starfleet cadets. While there he spent more time teaching cadets the intricacies of space flight and their duties as future Starfleet officers than he did in actual command.

The Vulcan put all of that aside when the Enterprise was needed to dissolve another galactic crisis, relinquishing his command to Kirk. Spock willingly returned to his role as second in command.

Spock and Riker are two of Starfleet's brightest lights. They are on a par at winning the respect and loyalty of their crews. Although their personalities are total opposites, each has the charisma that induces subordinates to follow their orders without question. Does this mean that they are cut from the same mold? Absolutely not!

STYLES OF COMMAND

Spock was born on Vulcan and is half human. Riker was born in Alaska on Earth and is all too human. Spock does not understand humor and wears a somber, some say grim, expression much of the time, while Riker has a ready smile, a hardy laugh and is quick with a joke.

Because of the nature of his race, Spock has superior intelligence and believes that all things can be solved by logic—or at least he did in his early years. More recent events have caused him to mellow that belief somewhat. Nor does he understand the human need for a thank you, or a pat on the back for a job well done. After all, that is what they are trained to do. So what if it was a desperate measure that saved

the ship from destruction with just seconds to spare.

Riker is quick with a compliment and believes it is good for morale for the ship's crew to be told their work is appreciated. He too is highly intelligent but leaves the serious logic and calculations to Lieutenant Commander Data, his android shipmate.

Surprisingly their boyhoods were not too different. Both were lonely, only children. It is true that Spock had a half-brother, Sybok. However he was much older and Spock saw little of him.

FAMILY PROBLEMS

Riker and Spock were both estranged from their fathers at a young age—Spock when he enrolled in Starfleet Academy against his father's wishes.

Riker's mother died when he was young, and his father, in his role as ambassador, would be gone for long periods of time and the boy felt abandoned. The two younger men each endured a period of approximately 15 years when there was no communication between themselves and their sires.

During their leisure hours Spock prefers to be alone or in the company of one or two people, usually Kirk and McCoy. Riker has a gregarious nature and enjoys crowds and parties. Spock enjoys chess. Riker prefers Poker. They do share an interest in music—Spock plays the Vulcan lyre, Riker the trombone.

Like Kirk, Riker has a lively interest in women and has had numerous short-lived love affairs. The one constant in his life in the affairs of the heart is Deanna Troi, the ship's Counselor. They were in love before either joined the Enterprise and now say they are just good friends—however there is a bond between them that transcends any new romantic interest either may have.

At the age of seven, Spock was bonded to T'Pring as is the Vulcan custom. When the time arrived for their marriage, T'Pring wanted another. With Kirk's help, and nearly at the cost of his life, the bond was broken. With the possible exception of the mysterious Romulan Commander and the spore-induced alliance with Leila Kalomi, Spock has shown little interest in romance.

THE SCIENCE OFFICERS

It is interesting to note that neither science officer is human—well Spock (23rd century) is half human, but he does his best to ignore that, after all his science ability and logic come from his Vulcan half.

And of course Data (24th century) is a construct, a machine—a computer in human form who wants to be completely human. And any captain in the fleet would give half a year's pay to have either one of them serving on his ship.

While it is true that Data is programmed with far more information than even a Vulcan mind can retain, in most ways the two are very similar. Each has super-human strength. Each has the ability to remember everything they learn, hear or see. Each are extremely loyal and obey orders without question. Both hold citations for gallantry, valor and the prestigious Legion of Honor. And each have a life span far beyond that of humans.

Like most Vulcans, Spock could live an active, useful life well past his 200th birthday. Data is programmed to continue as a functional android into infinity. They also have dual roles on the ship: Spock was Kirk's first officer and Data is Picard's helmsman. In addition, Data as second officer is third in command of the ship.

A FASCINATION FOR COMPUTERS

Perhaps their most common bond is their insatiable curiosity about life. The difference is how they go about satisfying this craving. Spock does quiet research, spending hours with his computer. Data is a computer so he asks questions, sometimes to the annoyance of his shipmates. His quest isn't so much for knowledge, he has that, but to learn all that he can about the human phenomenon.

Another bond they have is the one they would just as soon forget— each has a troublesome brother who, at their best, would be considered black sheep, and at their worst, nearly destroyed the Enterprise and crew.

Data and his evil brother Lore were the ultimate achievement of cyberneticist Dr. Noonian Soong, the man Data calls "Father." Data was discovered in a dormant state by the crew of the USS Tripoli on Omicron, the planet decimated by the Crystalline Entity (at Lore's instigation). When all contact with the Federation colony was lost, the Tripoli was sent to investigate. They found all life on the planet, including plants, had been eradicated. They also found the inert body that would eventually become Data. They took their find back to command headquarters where scientists discovered what he was.

Data has no knowledge of when he was created nor how long he remained in a dormant state before the Tripoli found him. Therefore much of his background is a mystery. After being declared a sentient being, Data was admitted to Starfleet Academy. He graduated four years later with many honors and degrees, including exobiology. He served on several ships, including the USS Trieste before transferring to the Enterprise.

Spock and Data are both well versed in the engineering arts and frequently worked closely with Scott and LaForge, the chief engineers, of their respective ships. They also share an active interest in the arts, including music. Data plays the violin and Spock the Vulcan lyre.

The helmsmen, the navigators and the engineers. These are vital positions often overlooked when discussing the more flashy and colorful rank and file members of the Enterprise teams.

Chapter Nine

THE SECONDARY BRIDGE CREWS OF THE ENTERPRISE

The Enterprise, which for 75 years has been the flagship of Starfleet, has retained its well-deserved reputation for being the pinnacle one could hope to achieve in star-ship duty. Captain Picard achieved it following a 22 year stint as captain of the Stargazer. Commander Riker achieved it following serving as first officer on another vessel and transferring to the newly completed Enterprise-D. Other crew members received similar promotions to the flagship of Starfleet.

In the 75 years between the Enterprise of the 23rd century and the Enterprise-D of the 24th century, various changes have been made so that while some key positions on the bridge and elsewhere have remained, others have changed and even been combined. The original Enterprise had a chief communications officer while the Enterprise-D has combined that duty with other functions.

In the days of Captain Kirk, it was not unusual to have the same crew throughout the entire life of his starship command. Other captains may have experienced more frequent personnel changes but that often was because of the captain involved and the ambitions of those who served under him.

Jean-Luc Picard has experienced the same sort of luck that James Kirk had in that his crew has remained largely intact during his seven years aboard the Enterprise. His only permanent loss was Lt. Tasha Yar who was killed in the line of duty.

BY JAMES VAN HISE

COMMUNICATIONS: LT. NYOTA UHURA

The only officer to serve as Kirk's communications officer on the original Enterprise was Lieutenant Nyota Uhura. Of course there were officers who served during the alternate shifts, or on the rare occasions when Uhura was assigned to a landing party, but during any critical situation, Nyota was the person Kirk wanted at that station.

She was an expert at understanding, and interpreting, obscure languages. Codes was another field in which she excelled. If another world developed a code that she couldn't break, it was unlikely that anyone, with the possible exception of Spock, could do so.

Following the completion of its five year mission under Captain Kirk, Uhura was rotated back to Earth where she served at Starfleet Command in her new rank of Lieutenant Commander. She remained in this role until summoned to the refitted Enterprise during what came to be known as the V'ger crisis. She remained under Kirk's command thereafter, through thick and thin.

Uhura knows whatever communications station she is working at both inside and out and can repair it even under the most demanding of combat situations.

LIEUTENANT WORF

As Security Officer on the Enterprise-D, Worf's duties include those formerly held to be the sole province of the communications officer. Besides communications, he's also in charge of tactical and makes certain the shields and weapons are always on line and ready to combat the unexpected.

Worf is the son of Mogh, born on the Klingon homeworld. Orphaned at the age of six on the planet Khitomer due to the Romulan massacre which took place there, the Klingon child was found and adopted by a human Federation officer and his wife. Returned to Earth, Worf was raised far from his own kind, but his foster parents did not shield him from his background. Rather Worf was raised to eat Klingon food and he learned about Klingon culture so that as an adult he would not be a freak among his own people.

This has produced a conflict in Worf. Even though the Klingons are at peace with the Federation and are active allies, they remain a warrior culture at heart. But because Worf was raised in the peace-loving Federation, he's had to deal with an

George Takei at the MANN's CHINESE THEATRE on December 5, 1991.

Photo by Chris Flicker

inner conflict this has produced. The Klingons venerate warfare and honor fighting above all else. So while Worf's human parents stressed peace, everything he learned about his native culture stressed warfare and battle.

This has produced an over-compensation in Worf. To prove that he is just as Klingon as the next warrior, he accepts without question everything his heritage teaches. Worf honors all aspects of his warrior background and reacts violently when he encounters Klingons who have turned their back on their culture, such as in "Birthright." Worf was so profoundly troubled by his encounter there that he immersed himself even more deeply in Klingon culture and took a leave of absence from the Enterprise to visit a planet considered holy to the Klingon people.

Worf was elevated to the position of Security Chief when Lt. Tasha Yar was killed on Vagra II. Worf had much admired Yar and feels honored to follow in the footsteps of someone who was killed in the line of duty.

While growing up, Worf believed he was the sole survivor of his family until he was visited by Kurn, who revealed himself to be Worf's brother. The Klingon brothers soon became involved in matters of intrigue on the homeworld, which ultimate led to them clearing their family name. Their dead father had been wrongly accused of consorting with the Romulans on Khitomer.

As if Worf's life weren't complicated enough, when a former lover, K'Ehleyr, is murdered, the Klingon Security Chief discovers that he sired a young son by her several years before. The child, Alexander, is first sent to Worf on the Enterprise. Not prepared for sudden fatherhood, Worf asks his foster parents on Earth to raise him. They try but realize they are too old to raise a Klingon youngster once again.

Returned to the Enterprise, the boy, Alexander, is at first resentful of his father, believing that he has already been rejected by Worf once already. The two have a difficult time adjusting to one another but finally reach an equilibrium in their father-son relationship.

THE HELMSMAN: LT. HIKARU SULU

Sulu originally joined the crew of the 23rd century Enterprise in the science department where he specialized in both physics and botany (a specialty of his parents).

During an intense combat situation when the Enterprise was under attack, the regular helmsman was injured and Sulu was pressed into service as the replacement. Although aware of what a helmsman was required, due to his training at Starfleet Academy, Sulu had never been tested under genuine combat conditions. He emerged a hero after guiding the Enterprise out of the way of another ship which was on a collision course.

Sulu and Kirk realized almost simultaneously that Hikaru's real talents were at the helm of the Enterprise, not hidden away in the science lab doing research and experimentation. Sulu had no objections to the promotion and transfer as the battle experience left him both shaken and energized. He's never felt more alive than when he had the control of the starship at his fingertips and knew that he had the skill to accomplish any task expected of him.

Hikaru had taken command courses in Starfleet but felt that the chance to command a starship was an unrealistic goal to aim at. Sciences seemed to offer a more secure future. But when fate stepped in and pressed him into duty, he knew that he couldn't turn his back on this opportunity to fulfill his secret dream.

Sulu had long wished for a command of his own but didn't believe it was possible in the highly demanding and competitive atmosphere of Starfleet. Now he knew differently. Sulu realized that not everyone had the aptitude for command that he had displayed, and Captain Kirk impressed this fact upon him when he offered Hikaru the promotion.

Years passed as Sulu remained on the Enterprise and was there when Kirk destroyed his beloved starship rather than allow it to fall into the hands of the Klingons. The fact that his captain had stolen the vessel in defiance of Starfleet orders seemed destined to mark the end of all of their careers, but as usual Kirk found a way out for all of them, and saved the Earth in the process.

Following their exoneration, Sulu served with Kirk for a time before being promoted off the Enterprise into the command of his own vessel, the Excelsior. Sulu's dream had been fulfilled, and one of his earliest missions as a starship commander was to Khitomer where he assisted the Enterprise in preventing an assassination that would have sabotaged the vital Klingon Peace Conference. The results of that conference changed the face of the Federation from that day forward as the cold war with the Klingons came to an end.

Commander Sulu and the Excelsior were now making their own legends.

COMMANDER DATA

Created by the reclusive cyberneticist, Dr. Noonian Soong, Data is the only android serving in Starfleet, but he is not the only one of his kind. Data is the second of his kind. The first, Lore, was created with human emotions, but Lore's emotions proved to be negative and destructive to human beings. Dr. Soong deactivated Lore and disassembled him. When he built Data he left out the emotions circuit due to the unpredictability of it.

Data was discovered by a Federation Away Team, but his creator had vanished. Returning to Starfleet, Data passed the enrollment requirements to join Starfleet Academy and completed his tasks along with his fellow human classmates. Upon graduation he was posted to a starship where he worked his way up through the ranks just like anyone else, finally achieving a promotion to the newly commissioned Enterprise-D.

It was on a mission aboard the Enterprise that brought them to the Omicron Theta star system and back to the world Data had been discovered. There, in Dr. Soong's secret laboratory, a double for Data was found carefully stored away. Upon assembling it, this duplicate seemed superior to Data in some ways, until it revealed its true evil nature. In the end Lore was beamed into space and apparently destroyed. Somehow he escaped and returned a few years later when Data was reunited with the aged Dr. Soong. Ultimately Lore managed to form an alliance with the Borg which almost resulted in Data's destruction.

Although an android who possesses super-human strength and a computer brain, he doesn't consider himself to be superior to human beings, such as Lore would. Data considered his inability to experience emotions a troubling state as he can only understand feelings such as love and hate as abstract concepts, not as sensations which control his decision making processes. But Data's constant association with humans has allowed him to come to understand how they would respond in certain situations and no one who knows him would describe the android as being cold or unfeeling. In fact he is quite the opposite as Data recognizes the power that emotions exert on people.

Data has achieved the rank of commander and looks forward to one day being granted a promotion to his own command of a starship. He was placed in temporary command of a ship, the Sutherland, during the "Redemption" incident and distinguished himself on the front lines in spite of having a first officer who didn't trust the android's abilities.

OTHER FACES AT THE HELM

Obviously the Enterprise, in its incarnations over the 23rd and 24th centuries, have had other steady hands at the helm. Miles O'Brien served as a helmsman when he was still an ensign. O'Brien was later promoted to Transporter Chief and finally was promoted off the

Enterprise entirely to become chief of operations on Deep Space Nine.

Geordi began his stint aboard the Enterprise working the helm, but he was soon promoted to engineering where he has excelled ever since. Geordi became the Chief Engineer when Lt. Commander Argyle was transferred to another vessel.

NAVIGATORS

It was during the second year of Kirk's five year mission that a new navigator transferred aboard the Enterprise, a young man named Pavel Chekov. A recent graduate of Starfleet Academy, Ensign Chekov had demonstrated keen navigation skills during tests he had undertaken at the Academy.

Pavel has no brothers or sisters and his parents are scientists whose work took them to many points around the galaxy during his childhood. He is from Earth and of Russian ancestry, a heritage his parents exaggerated somewhat in his eyes to the point that Pavel believed that all of the vital inventions in modern times came from Russia.

When he first transferred aboard the Enterprise, he was tested in many capacities before being assigned as the navigator. Later, after the Enterprise was reconditioned following the completion of its five year mission under Captain Kirk, Chekov was promoted to weapons officer.

Chekov followed in the footsteps of other navigations officers including Lieutenants Kelso, Farrell and Stiles. But Chekov impressed both Kirk and Spock the extent of his navigation skills. One of those previous navigators was Lt. Gary Mitchell (a friend of Kirk's since his academy days) who died tragically prior to Chekov's transfer to the Enterprise.

Following his promotion off the Enterprise to the science ship the Reliant, Chekov found himself encountering Khan, a 20th century criminal whom Jim Kirk had exciled to a distant world. Chekov's stint on the Reliant under Captain Terrell proved to be short lived when Khan captured the vessel and brought about Terrell's death while brainwashing Chekov with an especially torturous technique. It was only after Khan's destruction that Chekov rejoined Kirk's crew aboard the Enterprise.

Chekov's adventures with Kirk continued aboard the Enterprise-B when a new vessel was given to Kirk to command after he and his team (including Chekov) succeeded in saving the Earth by traveling in time aboard a captured Klingon ship.

Pavel remained with Kirk, surviving the near debacle of the Klingon Armistice at Khitomer to emerge on the heroic side once again.

THE 24th CENTURY ENTERPRISE

Picard has had a number of navigators since taking command of the Enterprise. These have even included acting ensign Wesley Crusher, prior to his leaving to attend Starfleet Academy. Wesley had to go far to convince Picard that he was the right boy, or man, for the job as Jean-Luc initially displayed irritation when he first discovered Wesley visiting the bridge. He didn't like children on his bridge. But he gradually came around as Wesley proved himself in certain vital incidents.

When Wesley left to attend the academy, a number of other officers stepped in to fill the post of navigator, none of whom particularly distinguished themselves until Ro Laren joined the ship's compliment. Commander Riker found her brashness and willingness to question her superiors an annoying trait, but Picard defended her assignment to the Enterprise, so Riker reluctantly accepted her.

Riker also disliked Ensign Ro because of her background. She had been court martialed and imprisoned after her failure to follow orders on an Away Team mission resulted in the death of eight crew members when she was serving aboard the Wellington. It was some time later that Admiral Kennelly commuted her sentence in return for helping him capture a Bajoran terrorist. The fact that Ro Laren is Bajoran herself made this a difficult offer to accept. Finally she realized that Admiral Kennelly was being tricked by the Cardassians and she confessed what she knew to Picard. As a result Ensign Ro was exonerated and Admiral Kennelly found himself facing a court martial this time.

Ro Laren remained aboard the Enterprise as navigator until the end of the Cardassian occupation of her home planet of Bajor. At that time she left the Enterprise to return home and help to rebuild her shattered life.

No permanent replacement has been made for Ensign Ro in the hope that she might some day return to duty aboard the Enterprise.

THE ENGINEERS: SCOTT AND LAFORGE

It has frequently been said that the captain may command a ship, but the engineers are the owners. Captains Kirk and Picard would certainly agree for their two Chief Engineers, Lieutenant Commander Montgomery Scott and Lieutenant Commander Geordi LaForge have each been responsible for yanking their ships from the jaws of destruction.

A starship engineer must be a mathematical genius. Scotty and Geordi are that and more. Each can be sound asleep, but let something go wrong with their engines, no matter how minor, and each is instantly awake and demanding to have the problem explained.

Scott was born in Scotland and entered Starfleet Academy at 18. After graduation he bounced from one small ship to another until he was assigned to the USS Constitution to help solve some of the many problems in engineering. He had even served for a time under Captain Christopher Pike, but it wasn't until Kirk became captain of the Enterprise that Scotty found a permanent home.

Kirk had recognized the genius in Scotty that others had missed and brought him aboard as chief engineer. Scott would remain on the Enterprise for the balance of his professional life—nearly 50 years.

Lieutenant Commander Scott was the right man in the right place at the right time. Although Earth had begun experimenting with space flight nearly 200 years earlier, the program was still in its infancy. Engines and equipment that worked in theory didn't work in practice—at least until Scott got his hands on them. He had the innate ability to take a piece of equipment that he'd never seen previously and soon have it functioning properly.

He took this ability with him to the Enterprise and it wasn't long until he'd earned the name "miracle worker." The crew doesn't like to count the number of times Scotty's quick thinking and "Rube Goldberg" tinkering in times of stress not only saved their lives but prevented the Enterprise from being blown to space dust. The engine room was his castle and he fiercely protected his beloved engines.

AN ENGINEERING MIRACLE

Lieutenant Commander LaForge was certainly as talented as his predecessor but in an entirely different way. Geordi's state-of-the-art engine room could, and did, make Scotty pop-eyed. Although there are times when Geordi had to depend on his own ingenuity, he also has a holodeck which he can use to call on the greatest minds in the galaxy to help him solve a problem.

Geordi's ability is all the more astonishing because he was born blind. Born in Earth's African Confederation, he lived quietly with his parents who had reluctantly accepted the fact of their son's blindness. However when he was about 5 years old he was caught in a burning building and, because of his lack of sight, could not escape unaided.

After his rescue, his terrified parents begged doctors to find a way to give him sight. There wasn't anything they could do to restore something he'd never had. But they could give him a form of sight. They devised a prosthesis they named Visual Instrument and Sight Organ Replacement (VISOR). This didn't give him what a sighted person would call normal, but it allows him to see much more and function better than the average person.

SCOTTY AND GEORDI MEET

While Scotty has sometimes been accused of sleeping with his engines, and sometimes he has had to, they aren't his only joy in life. He loves to have a "wee drop" with his friends from time to time. He also has a galaxy-wide reputation of making the best engine room hooch in the fleet.

Scott and LaForge had the unique experience of comparing their talents in person. Scott was a passenger aboard the transport ship Jenolen, on his way to the Norpin Five Colony and retirement.

After the Jenolen unexpectedly encountered a Dyson Sphere, the resulting crash left Scott the sole survivor. With just minutes of breathable air remaining, Scott rigged the Transporter pattern buffer into a continuous cycle hoping to remain alive until the ship was located. Little did he realize that time would stretch to 75 years, and his rescuer would be the Enterprise! Not his Enterprise, of course, but a new, much larger Enterprise.

He was thrilled at all the advances made since he had last presided over the engineering section of a ship. His joy was short lived when Geordi LaForge, this ship's Chief Engineer, wasn't interested in his suggestions or advice. That would all change when, at Captain Picard's suggestion, the two beamed down to the sphere's surface in an attempt to effect repairs on the Jenolen.

A NEW LIFE OF DISCOVERY

When the Enterprise-D was caught by a tractor beam and pulled into the Sphere's interior, it was left to Scott and LaForge to rescue them. Using a combination of Scotty's 23rd century by-the-seat-of-his-pants skills, along with Geordi's 24th century by-the-book approach, the pair was able to retrieve the Enterprise by the narrowest of margins.

In appreciation for his work in rescuing the Enterprise, Picard loaned the 147 year old engineer a shuttle craft in which to continue his journey, but the old space-dog decided retirement could wait. There was too much yet to learn and do.

A popular man, Scott enjoyed telling tall tales to his shipmates, in particular those just out of the Academy. But perhaps his greatest joy, other than his technical journals, was playing the bagpipes. No one who was at Spock's funeral will ever forget Scotty's soulful rendition of "Amazing Grace."

Scott had a tendency to spend many hours alone—but this had not always been true. As a youth and during his formative years as a Starfleet officer, his ruggedly handsome countenance, his happy disposition, was a combination few women could resist. The young man didn't lack for feminine companionship. When the girls learned they came in second, after his cherished engines, they usually wandered off in search of someone not quite so devoted to machinery.

THE LIGHTS OF ZETAR

Scott was in his middle years when the Enterprise was delivering new equipment to Memory Alpha, under the supervision of Lieutenant Mira Romaine. Mira and Scott were immediately attracted to one another. When her mind was possessed by the spirits of the last dead natives of the planet Zetar, Scotty was instrumental in saving her life.

Once her memory was complete, Mira continued on to her post on Memory Alpha, but the pair remained devoted to each other, spending shore leaves together whenever possible. It was rumored, but never confirmed, that the pair had entered into a contractual marriage. What is known—Scotty never again expressed an interest in another woman.

Unlike Scotty, LaForge has no desire to live his life alone for any reason, although his forays into the romance arena have been anything but a success. When complaining to Commander Riker about this lack of success, the first officer cautioned him to be patient, for when the right girl came along he would be glad he'd waited.

"Good advice," Geordi grumbled, after Riker was out of earshot, "but just what am I supposed to do in the meantime?"

Unlike Riker, Worf and other members of the crew, LaForge doesn't play a musical instrument, but he does enjoy music and can usually be found in attendance at shipboard concerts and stage productions.

One advantage the two engineers had in common that didn't change when the centuries did was the services of science officers who could, and did, frequently serve as extensions of the engineers own minds. Scotty had Spock, and Geordi has Data, to go beyond where their human minds can go.

Nichelle Nichols and Whoopi Goldberg at the Gene Roddenberry dedication.

Space, the final frontier, and not just for exploration but for space medicine as well.

The Enterprise is a starship at a time when alien races are commonplace with new civilizations being discovered on other worlds all the time. The expansion of human knowledge provided by these other worlds comes not just in the normal

Chapter Ten
EXOBIOLOGY: SPACE MEDICINE IN THE TIME OF STAR TREK

realms of scientific expertise, but in the medical arena as well. What do you do if a Vulcan catches a cold? What ailments are they subject to that humans are not, and are humans susceptible to alien diseases? In Ray Bradbury's book THE MARTIAN CHRONICLES, the native population of the red planet is all but wiped out by chicken pox brought to that world by one of the early expeditions.

Could ailments from other worlds wreck havoc on civilizations never exposed to them? Oddly enough, this is one angle pursued by STAR TREK only

in isolated cases. In "Miri" the landing party discovers that the world they've landed on was devastated by a biologically warfare plague centuries before which killed all members of the adult population when they reached maturity while retarding the aging process dramatically among the children. Kirk, Spock, McCoy and Yeoman Rand were exposed to the deadly contagion and it was up to Dr. McCoy to discover a cure for it before the disease could run its course in them.

In "The Deadly Years" another alien virus caused rapid aging, but McCoy was once again able to find a way to reverse it. Never addressed in this episode was that fact that any treatment which could reverse the aging process, whether it had been artificially accelerated or not, would be the basic research needed to retard the normal aging

The DeForest Kelley Star Ceremony held on December 18, 1991.

Photo by Chris Flicker

process as well. For all we know, Dr. McCoy discovered the secret to immortality in that episode.

AN OLD COUNTRY DOCTOR AND OLD COUNTRY ALIENS

Dr. McCoy referred to himself as an "old country doctor," but such standard physicians don't volunteer for duty which will bring patients across their table who bleed green and whose ancestors evolved from very different seas than humanity's did.

In "The Man Trap," Dr. McCoy had to try to treat Spock after he was attacked by a salt vampire. What saved Spock more than anything was that his body doesn't contain the same saline content of other beings, making him less than appetizing to the alien. McCoy knew he was in over his head with Spock. Spock may psychologically have a human side to him, but physiologically he's pure Vulcan.

McCoy's greatest medical challenge during that first year of the new five year voyage of the Enterprise under Jim Kirk was during "The Devil In The Dark" incident. When a silicon based, non-humanoid creature is injured by a phaser blast, McCoy is called upon to render medical aid. When the doctor sees the Horta, he can't believe his eyes. None of his deep space experience has prepared him for anything like this.

"You can't be serious," McCoy argues. "That thing is virtually made out of stone. I'm a doctor, not a bricklayer."

"You're a healer. There's a patient. Get to work and that's an order," Kirk states.

McCoy is skeptical but he gets to work, examining the Horta's wound and determining what, if anything, he can do. It's not even as though the Horta is an animal which he can call on veterinary skills for. It's a completely unknown type of creature. The fact that it's intelligent makes helping it all the more vital as the discovery of new life forms is one of the goals of the mission of the Enterprise.

Finally McCoy determines what he can use and has the Enterprise beam it down to him. When Kirk asks, "You mean you can help it?"

"Help it? I cured it! I had the ship beam down a hundred pounds of thermo-concrete, the kind we use to build emergency shelters out of. It's mostly silicon so I just troweled it into the wound and it'll act like a bandage until it heals. Take a look. It's good as new." And it was. McCoy's successful treatment of the Horta enabled that alien race and the miners of Janus VI to develop a partnership in which the Horta tunneled through rock and revealed mineral deposits for the miners to process, increasing their output a thousand fold.

A 24th CENTURY BEDSIDE MANNER

Having the last name Crusher must have proven an inopportune surname for Dr. Beverly Crusher. After all, the name does not imply a graceful manner. But Dr. Crusher's punishing sounding name has never been referred to in any of the NEXT GENERATION scripts, which is rather odd. I think were an average person to meet a doctor named Crusher that the name would be the first thing they'd remark on.

While Dr. Crusher had to come up with a cure for a malady in "The Naked Now" which was similar in many respects to what McCoy faced in "The Naked Time," she never had to trowel closed a wound on a silicon-based alien. Not only has she primarily dealt with humanoid types of aliens, but by the 24th century much more is known about non-human aliens.

The one time she's found herself up against the unknown was when Worf's spine suffered a crippling injury in "Ethics." That was when it was revealed that the medical computer only had limited information on Klingon physiology because in that culture, the concept of helping someone heal to the point where they would be alive but disabled goes against their cultural beliefs. Klingons believe that death is better than living as an object of pity. For this reason the medical research into crippling injuries among Klingons is virtually nonexistent. Klingons refuse to go on living as cripples.

What Dr. Crusher does know is that the Klingon body contains some duplications of functions, duplicate organs which act as a backup system should the primary system suffer injury. Thus when an experimental spinal cord replacement operation is done, Worf's biological backup systems kick in to allow the operation to be a success. Dr. Crusher learned as much from that one experience as she'd known about Klingon physiognomy to date. In fact, that operation provided medical breakthroughs which will be applied to the limited Klingon medical knowledge employed on their home world.

A DOCTOR WITH DETERMINATION

Although the Enterprise is run like a military vessel and McCoy takes orders from Kirk, he has no military rank. What he does have is the capability of certifying Kirk to be unfit for command should the circumstances so dictate. He can also recommend personnel for shore leave when their records indicate stress. McCoy designated Kirk as a candidate sorely in need of rest and relaxation in "Shore Leave" and Mr. Spock used McCoy's report to force Kirk to face that fact himself.

Although Dr. McCoy is more than willing to confront Kirk over his command decisions when they reflect on the crew, he is also the captain's close personal friend. It is because of this friendship that each feels free to openly state their opinions about any given situation. Thus when McCoy was hesitant about trying to treat the Horta, Kirk insisted because of his faith in his chief medical officer's abilities.

In the incident with "The Deadly Years," both Kirk and McCoy suffered debilitations from the ailment so that others had to deem Kirk unfit to command when the disease began to show its advanced stages in him. And yet even suffering from this, McCoy was still able to come through to help himself and his fellow officers.

CRUSHER AND THE ENTERPRISE-D

When Beverly Crusher was assigned by Starfleet to serve on the Enterprise-D, it would mark the second time that Jean-Luc had a Crusher under his command. When he was captain of the Stargazer, Jack Crusher, his close friend, served on the vessel. When Jack died during an attack on an Away Team, Picard took the loss personally and accompanied Jack's body back to Earth so that he could comfort the family himself.

Beverly found Jack's death hard to take. It took her some time to get over Jack's death enough to stop blaming his commanding officer, Jean-Luc.

Under Jean-Luc's command she has had the opportunity to bring her son, Wesley, with her so that their family was not divided the way it was when Jack Crusher served on the Stargazer. The Enterprise-D has been deemed an exploration ship as well as a ship of peace in the truest sense of the word. Larger than any Enterprise before it, the Enterprise-D carries a ship's compliment of 1,000, including the spouses and children of those stationed on board the flagship of Starfleet.

It was decided that with vessels going on extended journeys, sometimes lasting several years, that it would be better to be able to have crews bring their families along. In this way men and women wouldn't become stressed from prolonged separation from loved ones. Otherwise married personnel may have refused deep space assignments because of the time and distance involved from their homes. Since married personnel tend to be older and more experienced, it was desirable to have them along on the special assignments. In spite of the hazards this sometimes opens personnel up to, Beverly Crusher has never regretted bringing her son along.

THE STAND-IN DOCTOR

When Beverly Crusher received a special, temporary assignment back to Earth for a year, Wesley, who was already 16, decided to remain with the Enterprise. He had developed friendships with others on board and had been accepted by Picard as a useful member of the crew. So he remained when Beverly left the Enterprise.

Replacing Beverly was Dr. Katherine Pulaski, a career veteran with a great deal of deep space experience. Set in her ways, she knew what she was doing and didn't brook questioning of her expertise, particularly by an android.

Pulaski was suspicious of the android, Data, from the day they met. She couldn't understand how Starfleet could have given an android command rank and said as much. She believed that any human characteristics Data exhibited were strictly imitative, a matter Data disputed. Even though she clearly didn't like being around Data, the android wasn't offended since he didn't have any feelings she could offend.

Like Dr. McCoy, Pulaski was irascible and could be cranky about protocol and procedure. Also like McCoy, she disliked using the trans-porter but was more insistent at avoiding it than McCoy was.

When the crew of the SS Langtry was found dead of old age, Pulaski was on the job, tracing it back to the Darwin Science Station. It turned out that the children there have a genetic mutation which enables them to destroy a virus before it reaches their body. The presence in the area of a flu virus caused their bodies to create an antibody which was fatal to human beings not genetically altered the way the children are.

When Pulaski is exposed to this and begins aging, the children are quarantined at the Science Station while the adults are forced to leave them behind. Pulaski's ailment is cured when Picard, Geordi and O'Brien figure out how to use the transporter to recreate her genetic pattern prior to her exposure to the anti body and reintegrate the doctor's body the way it had been before. But because Pulaski had no exiting transporter records on the Enterprise, they had to improvise.

Pulaski soon found that she didn't really fit in with the other Enterprise personnel and was transferred to another vessel. This corresponded with Dr. Crusher's completion of her assignment on Earth and she returned to the Enterprise to be reunited with her son.

THE SHIP'S COUNSELOR

Another new addition to the Enterprise in the 24th century is the ship's counselor. Although doctors on starships have always had to play psychiatrist for their patients as well, the ship's counselor does this exclusively and their job is to observe personnel for signs of stress and job burnout. In particular she works with the command personnel since their decisions affect the rest of the crew.

Deanna Troi is half Betazoid/half human. A full Batazoid can read minds, but Deanna can only sense emotions and is a living lie-detector. She often stands at her captain's side during important meetings and negotiations and can quickly advise Picard when the person he is dealing with is lying or trying to hide something.

But Deanna can be tricked herself, such as when she fell in love with a negotiator at a conference being held on the Enterprise only to discover that he is a full Betazed. Thus the man can negotiate while secretly knowing his collaborator's every thought. Deanna felt that this was deceitful and their relationship fell apart over this matter.

One of her most difficult duties occurred when Sarek of Vulcan visited the Enterprise and she had to reveal her belief that the Vulcan was the source of the many problems the crew of the ship were experiencing.

Troi also chose to attend command school at the Starfleet Academy and has skills even beyond her inborn counselor abilities.

McCOY'S TRUSTED ASSISTANTS

Dr. McCoy dealt with the problem of having to treat Spock with his Vulcan anatomy when he brought on as his assistant one Dr. M'Benga. M'Benga was an expert in Vulcan anatomy and biology and was a vital consultant to McCoy on all matters relating to his science officer. As Kirk's first officer, McCoy's health was paramount. Since Spock remained secretive about such personal matters, McCoy didn't want to be surprised by another bout of pon farr or whatever else Spock might have percolating in his circulatory system that he considered too personal and private to discuss. McCoy hated being the last to know about the health of his crew.

The rest of the five year mission under Jim Kirk proceeded smoothly for McCoy and he returned to Earth where he intended to retire. He was somewhat taken aback when Starfleet informed him a few years later that he was being recalled to active duty—at the behest of Admiral James T. Kirk. McCoy angrily protested the situation at first, but secretly he was pleased to be reunited with his old friends. He was back aboard the Enterprise, ready to explore the reaches of space and encounter aliens he wouldn't know how to operate on again.

Leonard McCoy experienced a pleasant surprise when he discovered that Christine Chapel had earned a medical degree in the intervening years, with a specialty in alien anatomy. He bit back what he was thinking but privately knew that her interest had everything to do with Vulcan anatomy in particular, such as Mr. Spock's, for instance.

McCoy remained aboard the Enterprise with Kirk and had a chance to test his own increased knowledge of alien anatomy when a Klingon ambassador was attacked while space docked near the Enterprise and McCoy fought valiantly to save him. He didn't succeed, but he knew he had done his best. It took some time to convince the Klingons of that.

CRUSHER AND TROI

While serving as the ship's counselor and seeing to the mental health of the command crew, Deanna Troi also assisted Dr. Crusher. Troi would be present with Dr. Crusher during certain kinds of examinations, usually relating to people coming aboard the Enterprise from outside. In the case of examining wounded prisoners, Troi would be able to tell if the prisoner was faking their injury. It also made it harder for a child to pretend to be sick to avoid taking a test that day.

Deanna, and the rest of the Enterprise personnel, must contend with the periodic visits of her mother Lwaxana, who opposed her daughter's entrance into Starfleet and now tries to supervise her private life. At best Troi finds this to be a distraction as her posting to the Enterprise has opened up new vistas of learning and experience. She wants to be more than a ship's counselor as her abilities would also serve her in good stead in a command role.

Dr. Crusher was able to take advantage of the opportunities a starship offers when she met and fell in love with Odon, a Trill. The Trill are a long-lived race who can be transferred from one host body to another as they grow older. Dr. Crusher had an opportunity to perform a temporary transfer when Odon's host body was critically injured. Riker volunteered to host the Trill and Crusher performed the removal from the old host body into Riker's. It was the kind of rare hands-on training in space medicine one can only encounter aboard a space ship.

Crusher had an even stranger task to perform when an alien entered Troi's body and within hours Deanna delivered a child. They both knew that this couldn't be natural, but Troi bonded to it nonetheless. When the child chose to leave, Troi was devastated and Dr. Crusher had to try her best to comfort her.

Life in space produces demands on a physician that they can only sometimes imagine how to prepare for. McCoy found himself on the cutting edge, having to render his skills to Vulcans and aliens of many descriptions. Once he even had to perform an autopsy on a Tellerite. But every new experience was recorded for his professional descendants.

Dr. Crusher had the wealth of experience gained by McCoy and countless other starship medical personnel to draw from during her period of training several decades later. By then it was expected that a ship's chief medical officer would know how to minister to Vulcans and other prominent alien cultures in the Federation. Time changes knowledge and nothing changes faster or more completely than the practice of space medicine.

One of the prevailing undercurrents in the original STAR TREK was a healthy interest in the opposite sex, or was that an obsessive interest?

From the time of its birth to the present, STAR TREK has been one of the most popular shows ever, spawning books, conventions, movies and even a new series. There are different theories as to why this is so: its seriousness in tackling social issues, its wry, self-conscious humor, and its fun cheap-tech sci-fi sets and effects. But I have a feeling that STAR TREK's popularity is based on something more basic: It was and remains one of the kinkiest shows on television.

The general lasciviousness of STAR TREK is borne out by the existence of Trekkie writings that posit sexual relationships between the main characters, and a whole industry based around nude drawings of the leads. But these apocryphal works aren't necessary. To see some really weird sex, stuff that's strange on a

Chapter Eleven
LUST IN SPACE

deep psychological level, you don't have to go any farther than the show itself.

ROVING EYE

Let's begin with James T. Kirk, captain of the USS Enterprise and possessor of the worst Madonna/whore complex of the 22nd century. To the disappointment of the Enterprise's female personnel, Captain Kirk refuses to become involved with anyone because he's "married to his ship". But it's clear that the real problem is that he's emotionally incapable of having a mature male-female relationship.

Whenever Kirk does get it on, it's with some outrageously sexy bombshell who happens to be an alien—clearly nothing like Mom. And it always happens one of two ways: She seduces him, using some kind of magic alien love power (so he's not responsible) or he seduces her to save the ship (so it's all in the line of duty).

And it sure takes some high-powered witchery to get through to our hero's, um, emotions. Who can forget the immortal episode, entitled "Elaan of Troyus" (get it?), in which Kirk has to teach manners to a gorgeous yet savage queen so she can marry the ruler of the next planet over, thereby insuring peace throughout the solar system? They say that Troyian women's tears act as a high-powered love potion. Kirk is told it's only a legend. Elaan uses the height of feminine wiles to break down his guard: "Nobody likes me," she whimpers as a glistening salty droplet appears on her lovely cheek. Of course, the sympathetic captain just has to comfort her, to wipe the tear away—

Marina Sirtis at the Nikko Hotel as the cast of ST:TNG is honored by Education 1st.

Photo © 1993 Albert L. Ortega

and her sad expression instantly changes to a sly smile of triumph. "You cannot resist my love, my love," she taunts seductively (and poetically) in the midst of their embrace, and of course he can't—at least not until the end of the episode.

KIRK'S CONQUESTS

Other shows follow the same pattern. In one, a buxom, power-hungry medicine woman on an "underdeveloped" planet gets Kirk to breathe in the pungent vapors of the aphrodisiac plant with which she keeps her husband enslaved. In another, a blonde who takes an outer space drug to keep herself irresistibly beautiful tries to get information by whispering sweet nothings about how lonely a captain must get so far from home. . . What's a dedicated shipmaster to do?

On the other hand, when the captain's in a nasty fix, the party of intergalactic bad guys usually includes a female upon whom Kirk can use the ol' Earthman charm. More than likely she's a robot or alien gal who's never experienced human passion before—and Jim's just the one to show her what she's been missing. Just one caress on the shoulder and she goes limper than if he had applied the Vulcan Nerve Pinch. I never thought it could be this way, she says, and before you

know it the Enterprise is soaring back out into the Final Frontier.

Of course, Kirk does fall in love from time to time. All it takes is a woman so unsullied and pure that snow would seem colorized by comparison. Naturally, she manages not to cramp his style or interfere with his relationship with the mother ship—instead, she courteously dies by the end of the episode. For instance, there's the time he flips over Joan Collins, playing a peacenik on the order of Gandhi (who, even in his younger days could never have made the cover of PLAYBOY). Alas, the space gang has time-traveled into the past, and Collins is slated by fate to walk in front of a truck. Kirk can't even stop her—that darned duty again!

Kirk really goes head-over-heels for a girl who could have been born yesterday—in fact, she's an android and she was born yesterday. He realizes that stunning, brilliant 20-year-old appearing virgins are in great demand just about anywhere in the known universe, and he makes a heavy play for her, but she can't decide between him and her immortal, thousand-year-old creator, with whom she has a "father-daughter" relationship. Built to withstand everything except Oedipal neurosis, the winsome girloid short-circuits right out of Kirk's life. Oh well, time to shoot the ol' ship back into deep space.

VULCAN RITUALS

Sure, you say—but what about Mr. Spock, lusted after by women of 10 galaxies as the ultimate Unattainable Man? Just how repressed is he?

Spock is half human, but he's also half Vulcan, and the Vulcan half rules. Vulcans are creatures of perfect rationality and no emotion, so as long as Spock's Vulcan half is in control, he reasons entirely with his head. (This makes him the perfect counterpoint to Kirk, who usually thinks with his, er, intuition.)

Spock is so ice-cold that he only needs to have sex once every seven years—and when the time finally comes, he misses out. His Vulcan bride has decided she'd rather have someone who actually lives on the planet. But does Spock care? "Negative, Captain," he says in the steely monotone of the man born to direct STAR TREK III.

The intriguing thing, and, to many viewers, the sexy thing about Spock is that you get the impression that his Vulcan side is holding his human side down somehow—that somewhere below all the rationality is a boiling cauldron of raging emotions. Who in this alienated world of ours can't identify with that? And we get to see plenty of instances in which the cauldron is caused to overflow. Usually, as with the freeing of Kirk's libido, some insurmountable outside force is required.

THE SPOCK TOUCH

Perhaps we should start with those alien spores, the ones that give people a peaceful easy feelin' whether they want it or not. Spock is introduced to them by a country gal (why don't these women leave the guys alone?) who happens to like the shape of his ears. He tries to fight it, but the spores are too much for him. Suddenly, Spock the untouchable becomes Leonard Nimoy the poet. (Really—check your bookstore).

Or how about when Spock and McCoy go way back in time, back to the point where Vulcans were still savages—and for some reason Spock starts slowly turning into a savage, too? It just so happens that they're stuck in a cave with a brilliant, lonely time-travelin' girl who, strangely enough looks exactly like Mariette Hartley did in 1967. Savage Spock knows what he wants, and it ain't logic. It's too bad they have to escape without her, but Spock wouldn't have been any fun when he was back to normal anyway.

Strangely enough, Spock's unleashed emotions never lead him to unleash anything else—even when he loses his logic he keeps his chastity (although he does get into some heavy finger-touching with a lady Romulan). To this very stardate, he may never have had a chance to have spent his seed anywhere it could have a chance to bear part-human, part-Vulcan fruit.

FUTURE TREK

Of course, the rest of the crew get to have their peccadilloes, too. There's two sights, for instance, that could never be erased from our personal logs: young Ensign Chekov simultaneously giving away and forgetting the secret instructions for flying the ship as his Russian hippie ex-girl friend makes goo-goo eyes at him, and Scotty going crazy out of his mind in infatuation with a head-turning crewperson who ends up falling for the Greek god Apollo.

In fact, what is it with these power-crazed women? When they're not seducing men with ulterior motives in mind, they're making out with some god, or a guy being turned into a god by an alien force or a villain (the young Ricardo Montalban, to be exact) who looks like a god. Is there something Gene Roddenberry is trying to tell us here?

Maybe so. After all, "The Cage" (the original pilot episode which featured a mostly different cast), is little more than a series of seduction fantasies. See, there's this beautiful woman being held in a zoo by telepathic aliens, and she needs a mate. . .

STAR TREK—THE NEXT GENERATION has dropped a lot of hints but has largely portrayed its cast as being chaste, if not downright sexless. Picard and Beverly circled each other a couple times, but it never went anywhere. Riker and Troi had been lovers discreetly offstage before the series began, but that's all over now. Riker did seem to be on the verge of pushing the edge of the envelope in "Angel One" when he had to dress up as a boy toy, but it was strictly in the line of duty.

Riker did once demonstrate, though, that he was as libidinous as any Classic Trek 23rd century officer. In "The Game," when he is in the presence of a young woman who is clearly there to make his shore leave memorable, Riker leers at her like she's a 110 pounds of pretty meat! It proved that 24th century man isn't so different from 20th century man after all, which was apparently the point.

Meanwhile, Worf has been in seven years of self-denial, and even when teenage Wesley was on board the boy's hormones were so quiet and under control we had to believe that his mother was slipping him something in his orange juice.

BACK TO BASICS

I expected that the new STAR TREK series would be relatively free of the dated '60s sexism that mars the old one. Unfortunately, with one exception, THE NEXT GENERATION also lacks the weird Freud-laced sexuality that makes the old one so great.

The one departure from that, which occurred early on when Gene Roddenberry was still rewriting episodes, was in "The Naked Now." Under the influence of some wild space sickness, Tasha Yar drags Data into her quarters to do the humpty-dance, only the garnish is that Data isn't human. Perhaps that was supposed to be the point—that Tasha Yar had never found a man who could satisfy her and had always secretly believed that Data could finally hit the spot.

It's a cinch that in an age when people are afraid to do it with their next door neighbor, much less a seductive Grabax from the Andromeda nebula, these voyagers will be keeping their spaceballs to themselves (unless a willing, sterilized android happens by).

And that's too bad. We'll just have to keep watching the reruns. . . like the one where Kirk is forced to switch bodies with a former girl-friend. Now there's a kinky show!

Wearing uniforms which seemed to stress individuality over conformity, the Enterprise crew of the Mirror universe were a force to be reckoned with. Much can we perceive from what was portrayed in the Trek Classic episode "Mirror, Mirror". This is the first in what will be a detailed, on-going series.

Chapter Twelve
LIFE IN THE MIRROR UNIVERSE

Space, the final frontier for manifest destiny. Once the Earth was united under an emperor it was decided to expand the empire. The stars held boundless possibilities for conquest. The united nations of the Earth worked in congress to advance the cause of space flight. An important advance in the cause of interstellar expansion came in the year 2003 when a starship from Vulcan visited Earth.

Cold, calculating, cruel and exciting. This is life in the mirror universe.

The Federation of our universe is the Empire of the mirror universe. It's as though the Federation had changed places with the Klingons. Cruelty replaces kindness. Assassination is fueled by ambition.

Only the strong and the cunning survive.

This is the realm into which James Tiberius Kirk was born. As a youth, Kirk soon became known as Tiberius and his peers recognized him as the dominant force in his group.

Starfleet came to grade schools to test children and determine their suitability as warriors. Ten year olds were tested for fitness as well as their tolerance to pain and humiliation. But Tiberius Kirk stood up to it all, even the tests that left his classmates terrified and in tears. Tiberius just laughed. The Starfleet examiners gave young Kirk high marks for his performance and instructed the school to place him in accelerated courses.

If Tiberius had been cocky before, he was insufferable now. His teachers found this an encouraging sign. By the time he was 15 Tiberius was ready for Starfleet Academy. The friends he'd grown up with had been left far behind. Tiberius Kirk was his own man.

THE MENACE OF FINNEGAN

In the academy he excelled in his courses, particularly in the History and Execution of Assassinations. He could name every U.S. President and when they were assassinated. His favorite was JFK who lived through 5 complete terms, thwarting 7 assassination attempts, including the one by his vice-president, Lyndon Baines Johnson, at the launch of Apollo Eleven. There in the sealed presidential box, JFK himself wrestled the gun from LBJ's hand and executed him on the spot while the secret service agents loyal to JFK or LBJ shot it out.

Tiberius found history to be very illustrative of life as he knew it. It was survival of the swiftest. Life was for the fleet and nimble of mind. You had to have an edge, an angle, if you were going to make it to the top and stay there, otherwise your life was just another rung in somebody else's ladder.

In the Academy the upper classmen took particular relish in making life miserable for the fresh-

men. One in particular, named Finnegan, zeroed in on Kirk. Kirk never budged or showed any anger over the pranks and petty humiliations Finnegan managed to wreck on him. But this was life and Kirk accepted it.

The fact that Tiberius Kirk was arrogant and self-involved made it difficult for him to make friends, not that he cared. Friends could be a liability once one achieved any sort of position of power in the Empire. But Kirk did manage to befriend one Gary Mitchell, a man who saw what Kirk had the makings of and knew he could benefit from the association in the long run. Kirk understood why Mitchell had befriended him but he didn't mind; it would become important to have someone he could trust to watch his back.

NOT A MAN TO BE CROSSED

Finnegan saw Mitchell as a weakness he could exploit to get to Kirk. When Finnegan staged an accident which seriously injured Mitchell, Kirk returned the favor during a simple outing when a transporter chip malfunctioned just as Finnegan was beaming up to Starfleet Academy's orbiting space station training platform. Finnegan vanished, atoms and all, never to be found again.

Kirk's classmates knew he was behind it and his standing increased enormously as a result. Even Finnegan's cronies steered clear of him, realizing that Kirk was more ruthless and clever than Finnegan ever imagined himself to be.

Tiberius graduated with honors and was posted to a starship. His skills and daring in combat caused him to quickly elevate in rank until he was transferred to the Enterprise. When several crewmen died on a planet because Captain Pike failed to recognize the threat they obvious posed, Kirk assassinated Pike and became captain.

When the Enterprise answered a distress call to Talos IV, Tiberius was suspicious. When he pierced the hoax of the survivors' encampment, Kirk quickly destroyed all signs of life on Talos IV due to the threat a race with such powers posed.

The Enterprise of the Mirror universe is a deadly place.

Lt. Sulu as head of security, employs tactics reminiscent of the ancient Gestapo. Mr. Spock, a bearded Vulcan, comes from a planet whose people were known for their viciousness. When he felt encroached upon by Sulu's watchful eye, he reminded the Security Chief that were anything to happen to him that he would be revenged by his operatives, some of whom are Vulcans. The implication was clear—Vulcans were dangerous, alive or dead.

This is a universe very different from that of the Federation, and future articles will explore this strange and fascinating realm in even more devastating detail.

Part Two—
BEHIND THE SCENES

It was 1991 and a particularly interesting time for the actor who plays William Riker to be making convention appearances. He had recently appeared on THE ARSENIO HALL SHOW and gleefully remarked on how weird STAR TREK fans are. . .

Chapter Thirteen

JONATHAN FRAKES: WILL RIKER SPEAKS

Jonathan Frakes made a convention appearance October 4-6, 1991 at the OCTOBER TREK convention. During his opening remarks he greeted the audience and said "Hello" from everyone in the cast of STAR TREK—THE NEXT GENERATION. When referring to Brent Spiner, he mentioned that Brent had just come out with his first album, "Old Yellow Eyes Is Back."

"Brent is out on the Con circuits these days," Frakes added. "He might even dance for you!" Jonathan also offered best regards from Captain "Pecan," the wackiest nut in the galaxy, which is the nickname given by the cast to Patrick Stewart. Frakes mentioned that Patrick would soon be doing his Broadway play, a one-man-show based on A CHRISTMAS CAROL in New York City in December. He encouraged everyone to see "old baldy" do his Christmas stories, and mentioned that cast members teased Patrick Stewart about his Pontiac commercials. Jonathan quickly illustrated by imitating, in a most serious British accent, the advertising slogan: "Pontiac—the American Car!"

Jonathan revealed that Gates McFadden had recently had a bouncing baby boy named James McFadden Talbot. "He's a beautiful baby, too. Did anybody figure out that she was pregnant during the filming? Well, I hope not because the directors meticulously filmed her from angles that would not reveal it by using mostly 'back' and 'head and shoulders' camera shots."

Frakes revealed that lovely amzadi, Marina Sirtis, and turtlehead

BY DIANA COLLINS

Michael Dorn, send their regards as well and that they're also doing the convention circuit. "In fact, Michael is at a convention in Hawaii right now. Don't we feel sorry for him? I hope you'll get the chance to see them at other conventions soon!"

The actor was generous in his compliments of his fellow performers, and added, "Colm Meaney did a fabulous job acting in the movie THE COMMIT-MENTS." He also mentioned that Meaney was also doing a film with Daniel Day Lewis.

Patrick Stewart

Photo © 1993 Albert L. Ortega

FUTURE TREK

As to future episodes, Jonathan mentioned that Michelle Forbes was joining the cast as a semi-regular. "She's a rebel-type character, Ensign Ro. Coincidentally she's the same actress that played the daughter of the doctor who had to kill himself at age 60 in 'Half A Life.' Didn't David Stiers and Majel Barrett perform wonderfully in that episode? Majel will be back, of course. Also Worf's son, Alexander, will be back."

What about the frozen "pop-cycle people" last seen in "The Neutral Zone," someone wondered? "Yeah, I wonder what happened to them myself. I don't know of any upcoming scripts that highlight their return, however."

Someone also wanted to know if Kyle Riker, Will's father, would be seen in any forthcoming episodes. "I don't know right now, but I'd like to see Mitchell Reiner make another appearance. He was fun to work with."

Actress Susie Plaxon was popular as she played a Vulcan, Dr. Selar, as well as Worf's Klingon lover. But since Worf's girlfriend died, it was asked whether Susie might return as Dr. Selar? "I think so," he said, "but not in the near future."

PERSONALLY SPEAKING

When asked if Frakes is originally from Pennsylvania, he replied in the affirmative. "Yes, my folks still live in Bethlehem, Pennsylvania. I was born in Belfont, Pennsylvania and grew up in State College and attended Penn State University."

On some personal matters, Frakes is more reticent, such as

when asked about his height and his age. "Six feet four inches and I won't tell my age, thank you very much."

Just as the other actors have been asked at various conventions, Jonathan Frakes was asked whether he'd like to ride the Space Shuttle if NASA offered him the opportunity.

"Yes, in a minute!" he replied. "I think the powers that be probably have many more famous and deserving people who'll get a shot at it long before I'm called, including the original STAR TREK cast."

When a fan announced that NEXT GENERATION was the first show she'd seen him in and that she really liked Jonathan's acting, he was flattered. "Well thank you very much for the compliment! Actually I've played in several bit roles here and there, mostly as the villain of the week. It's nice to play more of a good guy major character role."

WEIGHING IN

From seemingly left field came a question regarding whether the actor weighed the same now as he did in the first season? This may have been inspired by the fact that as the original STAR TREK series progressed in the 1960's, star William Shatner tended to put on weight during the year to the point that he'd have to diet between seasons to get back in shape again. This is even detailed in the book THE MAKING OF STAR TREK in memos from Gene Roddenberry referring to the matter of William Shatner's "equator."

But regarding Jonathan's equator, he seemed to answer the question but didn't get real specific. "I absolutely love to eat as much as I absolutely hate to exercise. So in order to maintain bulk in the uniform, I eat pizza, junk food—you name it. Also my wife and I live on two coasts; she's in New York acting in the soap scene while I'm in L.A. doing STAR TREK—THE NEXT GENERATION. So I don't eat the foods I should because she's not around to save me from my bad eating habits."

Jonathan Frakes has never hidden the fact that the inventive rationales sometimes put forth to explain things which happen in the plots sometimes baffle him. So when he was asked how it was that Denise Crosby was going to come back to NEXT GENERATION after having died in two different episodes, he replied, "I don't fully understand the logic myself. But somehow in that alternate universe episode, 'Yesterday's Enterprise,' Tasha decides to stay to fight on that other Enterprise ship and gets captured and ends up having a daughter born half-Romulan. It's all very complicated because Tasha is approximately Riker and Worf's age, but then we see Tasha's child, Seela, in 'Redemption,' who is also our age. Then again, time warp theory is not part of my script. You'll have to ask someone more knowledgeable on the subject, such as the writers. All I can ask is how many times is this woman going to die?"

When reminded of the scene in "First Contact" with Bebe Neuwirth, Frakes laughed and said, "It was a really funny scene! She's a very talented actress!"

CANDID COMMENTS ABOUT CONS

It was inevitable, though, that someone would ask Jonathan about a then recent appearance on THE ARSENIO HALL SHOW in which the actor talked about how "weird" the STAR TREK fans we're that he'd seen at conventions.

"That was a mistake," he admitted. "I shouldn't have said that. I put my foot in my mouth. You know what I mean? I tend to have foot-in-mouth disease when talking to the media. So I want to apologize right here and now. I've had other moments of foot-in-mouth disease. For example, once I stated in a fan magazine that the reason why I kept turning down captain's positions was because of bad writing, which went over 'real well' when Michael Piller and Ron Moore saw it. I wasn't very popular with them for quite awhile after that one."

Regarding conventions, Frakes related what his first experience at one was like. "My first guest appearance at a convention was in Syracuse, New York during the first season. When I went into the Dealer's Room, I discovered most of the dealers were blatantly giving away Riker action figure dolls for free if customers bought any other figure. Also I noticed that the dolls of Data and Tasha were going for big bucks, some of them $200+. So I began to wonder if it would become the story of my life: buy an action figure, get Riker free."

Frakes was asked whether personally, and as an actor, if it transcends his individual involvement when he goes to conventions to see the fans?

"It's a treat to be on STAR TREK—THE NEXT GENERATION, especially after playing rapists, drug dealers and assorted unsavory characters. It's nice to know that I'm getting up every day to a good job and going to work with Patrick Stewart, Brent Spiner and the rest of the cast."

ANDROID OBSERVATIONS

Asked whether the actor thought that Data made a good captain in the episode "Redemption," he replied, "Yes, Data did real good as a captain after all! Oh, that guy playing his first officer certainly hated him, didn't he? I personally liked seeing Data as my first officer and Picard as an Admiral as in 'Future Imperfect.' "

Another Data question dealt with the different way the character has been described over the years of the series. Originally he was referred to as being a bio-mechanical life form who both Dr. Crusher and Geordi would work on, but lately only Geordi would work on the android's repairs as though he's just a tin can with circuits. Frakes pondered that a moment and then observed, "Data is already pretty human, isn't he? But that's a good point now that you mention it." But even if they had asked Brent Spiner that question he might not have been able to do anything about it any more than Jonathan Frakes can.

When asked what his favorite episode of NEXT GENERATION is, the answer landed on the character of Data once again. "That would be '1100101,' and of course 'The Offspring,' a Data episode that I was lucky enough to direct. My first directing experience," he added. "Since then I've directed another one and am promised more after that."

Regarding what it was like to direct his peers, the actor stated, "I was very lucky to get a Spiner show. Although we don't get to pick the script we direct, Rick Berman assigned me one that was a really good script to work with. Naturally the cast played with me a little bit at first, like they would refuse to come out of their dressing rooms when they were supposed to, to test me, and so forth."

But when Patrick Stewart directs him, Jonathan finds that he's the subject of some unique requests. "I've had to reshoot a lot of scenes because I smile too much. Patrick keeps telling me, 'Don't flare your eyes. . . don't smile. . . use that famous mid-western squint when you look at the camera."

FUTURE SEX

Another wild question emerged which started out sounding quite legitimate. A fan observed that Riker is a very romantic character and she wondered how many illegitimate children Commander Riker probably has by now? Frakes was taken aback and proclaimed,

"I'd like to think that Riker practices safe sex!"

Speaking of sex, in the episode "The Host" an alien entity temporarily occupied Will Riker's body, during which time Dr. Crusher carried on an affair with the alien. But what the fans wanted to know was how they made the character Odon appear to expand and contract in his abdomen when Dr. Crusher was doing the initial transplant?

"That was one of Michael Westmore's famous special effects," Frakes explained. "Michael was actually lying under the medical bed blowing up a balloon, then pumping a small amount of air in and out of the balloon to simulate movement as if there was something alive inside me. The whole procedure was very entertaining for everyone to watch on the set. Michael Westmore is an incredible genius! And his son, who works with him, creates those fabulous electronic light show effects, such as when Data's head gets opened up, as it has so much lately."

LAUGHTER ABOARD THE ENTERPRISE

Mistakes, out-takes and the STAR TREK blooper reel has been a popular item with fans since it first surfaced in the '70s. A NEXT GENERATION blooper reel has been seen at conventions, so Frakes was asked about what kind of pranks the actors play on set? Jonathan described the antics of two of the biggest tricksters in the cast.

"The most absurd thing on the Enterprise is to see Brent Spiner and Michael Dorn do dueling Gregory Peck impersonations. Brent also does Jimmy Stewart impressions. Michael and Brent perform this duel by finishing each other's sentences."

Another incident he described involved the episode "Skin of Evil." "It was pretty funny when during Tasha's holodeck epitaph and farewell scene, Patrick Stewart and all are walking towards the spot where the scene is to be shot in this rolling green valley. Suddenly Patrick breaks out into song: 'The hills are alive with the sound of music!' " But the cast have other interesting quirks as well. "Patrick, when he's doing a scene and gets caught chewing gum, will stick it behind his ear.

"Also, ever since we finished our singing debut on Brent's album as the Sunspots, we've begun entertaining the cast and production staff with those songs between takes."

People also want to know about Riker, such as what the "T" in William T. Riker stands for. "Now let's see," Frakes replied, considering. "Captain James T. Kirk's middle name is Tiberius, right? Well, I'm not sure exactly, but I'd like to think it was Thelonius, after the monk."

UNIFORM CONCERNS

Asked what he doesn't like about doing NEXT GENERATION, Jonathan said, "The only thing that I, and Patrick also, don't like about the job is the spacesuit (referring to his uniform). Have you all seen and like Patrick's new captain's jacket? Doesn't he look like Ike Turner in that thing?" Regarding the uniforms, Frakes added, "The uniforms are so hot that they have to be changed and washed, sometimes several times per day. They also fit so tightly that the seams start to give after a short while. Whenever that happens, I put my fingers in the loose spot and pull until the seams rip out. Unfortunately it's not a big hit with the costume department. Fortunately the new two-piece uniforms allow the body heat out in the middle."

Asked about a possible NEXT GENERATION movie, Frakes mentioned that he hoped to see one soon after the sixth season, although as it turns out the TNG film will go into production right after the conclusion of the seventh season of the series.

Guinan has remained largely a mysterious character ever since she was introduced in the second season of NEXT GENERATION. Asked whether the nature of Picard's relationship with Guinan will ever be revealed, Jonathan said, "Well, we know that Guinan is about 700 years old and their relationship has been stated as 'closer than friends.' There will be an episode this season which will go into their past relationship." That, of course, referred to the episode we now know as "Time's Arrow."

And what is Whoopie Goldberg like to work with? "Patrick described Whoopie as, 'No matter what kind of day you're having, when you see her, you'll see it improve dramatically.' We affectionately call her 'Shuttlehead' because of her huge hats."

PRE-TREK ROLES

One of Jonathan Frakes more prominent roles in the pre-TNG days was on the mini-series NORTH AND SOUTH. Regarding whether a sequel to that mini-series might ever be produced with the same characters from the original returning, the actor observed, "Well, that's entirely possible for me since my character was still alive at the end of NORTH AND SOUTH. Of course, being dead didn't stop Denise Crosby from coming back, did it?

"Seriously, yes. I'd be interested in doing a sequel once my STAR TREK—THE NEXT GENERATION contract runs out, and with Genie (Francis) of course. Have you ever seen Genie on TV? She has had a large fan following since she was quite young. Reprising Pat Swaizie's role might be a little expensive, now."

Regarding whether his wife, Genie, is ever going to make an appearance on NEXT GENERATION, Jonathan stated, "I don't know, but it's sort of a curse to be Riker's girlfriend, isn't it? He either kills her or she ends up dead, killed by a giant snowflake or some terrible thing."

RIKER'S LOVE LIFE

A facet of Riker's character that had been introduced early in the series but never pursued was his past involvement with Counselor Troi. On the subject of whether this would ever be dealt with in a more involved manner, Jonathan stated, "We aren't letting the writers get away with not having or showing some feelings for each other on the show. But it's their decision not to keep our relationship too strong in order to allow other love interests to occur for both of our characters."

Asked if he objected to getting all of the women on NEXT GENERATION, Jonathan laughed and said, "Yeah, it's really rough. No, actually I can't complain a bit!"

In "The Best of Both Worlds," Riker became commander of the Enterprise, if only temporarily. Concerning whether he was happy when Picard was captured because of how it advanced the character of Riker into a more prominent role, Frakes explained, "It was fun doing the Borg episodes because Patrick had to arrive at the studio about 3:00 AM to have makeup artist Michael Westmore apply tubes and other mechanical paraphernalia, which had to be glued onto his neck and other body parts.

"Also, I kind of liked Data as a first officer and Picard as an admiral, as they were in 'Future Imperfect.' But does it make sense to be a captain on a ship when there's no series attached?"

A GROWING CONCERN

A fellow trombone player asked Frakes if he really enjoyed playing the instrument and who his favorite musician was on the trombone?

"Actually that was one of the things the writers allowed me to add to the show. I began to play trombone in the fourth grade because I had long enough arms to reach all the note positions. I'm a real fan of Jack Tiegart."

Then there's the matter of Riker's beard, which Jonathan has had since the beginning of the second season of NEXT GENERATION. As to whose idea it was, he admits that it was his.

"I decided to grow it during the hiatus. When it was time to begin the season again, I proposed the idea to the staff and they didn't like it at first. But Gene Roddenberry thought it over, since old sea captains customarily wore beards. Gene decided to try trimming it to determine if it could look acceptable. So I sat in a dressing room chair, fully expecting to have him slowly trim the whole thing off eventually. He trimmed and he trimmed. Finally, after one-third of the growth had disappeared, he seemed satisfied with what was left. Then after the first episode with my beard, Gene sent a memo ordering them to cut the beard down another two percent! I felt fortunate to keep it!"

THE ENTERPRISE

Frakes was asked which kinds of shows he preferred doing—the "bottle" shows (which take place entirely on the Enterprise) or the "planet hell" shows?

"I think that most of us prefer the planet hell episodes because we get to do more exciting things, like when I had to dunk myself in that black slime pit, and when I got to eat live grubbs. I am elected to do those kinds of things because it goes along with my 'get Mikey to do it' image."

Which brings up what it's like working in Metamucil, black printer's ink and such on the set? "I feel a lot like Mikey. When we were filming that scene, LeVar Burton leaned over me and said, 'Ohhh, I'd never do that!' "

But Frakes admits there have been times when he's drawn the line on what he's willing to do for the show. "In the episode where the crew has hallucinations from REM sleep deprivation, there's a scene where I have snakes crawling all over my legs and feet in bed. I chose not to do that stunt! No one else wanted to stand in for me either! So the snake wrangler agreed to put his feet in the snakes."

BEHIND-THE-SCENES

One of the recurring complaints cast members had early in the run of NEXT GENERATION was with the scripts, although they never went public with their complaints. Fans did hear behind-the-scenes stories though. When asked whether he and Patrick Stewart have seen any positive effects from changes in the writing staff, Jonathan stated, "The first couple of years there were 25 writers going through a revolving door. The stability of the latest team of writers has made a world of difference in the quality of the shows. We believe that they are deliberately keeping us out of the loop, and the writers believe that we take far too much interest in their scripts."

A common question that many fans have wondered about is why the Emmy Awards have consistently failed to nominate any of the actors on NEXT GENERATION. "They should," Frakes stated. "This year especially Patrick should, and Brent should have been nominated for 'Sarek' and 'Brothers' (respectively). The original show tried to make nominations but the rules in NATUS don't include a STAR TREK kind of category of show—science fiction rather than sitcom. I certainly don't understand their reasoning."

On how long it takes to film an episode, the actor explained, "Seven days—eight days for the difficult ones, and we get our scripts on day six for the next episode."

Another behind-the-scenes fact came out when Frakes was

asked if it was true that he wore a pink chenille robe in his trailer. "Yes, " he confirmed, "but it disappeared one day."

FUTURE CONCERNS

Asked whether NEXT GENERATION would be open-minded enough to air an episode dealing with the gay, or sexually challenged persons in the 24th century, Frakes revealed, "There's a gay storyline episode planned in the future." This was, of course, "The Outcast" which was seen in the fifth (the 1991-92) season.

But what would Jonathan Frakes like to see more of in the future on THE NEXT GENERATION? "I'd like the stories to have more humor, more songs, more Klingon women, more 'Gahh' [Klingon wiggling worm food], and especially more irony."

The Borg never fail to elicit audience questions because so little is known about this strange and deadly race. For instance, while Borg nurseries have been seen, Borg women seem to have been scarce.

"There were some women who played Borg in the 'Best of Both Worlds' episodes. They're harder to distinguish with all of those tubes and mechanical devices sticking out, plus the stark white makeup."

OF FANS AND KLINGONS

When fans write to stars, they're not always certain that the performer will personally see the letter. But Jonathan Frakes assured his audience that he sees everything. "Nothing gets diverted elsewhere. We've all been advised that it's a very good idea to read all of our fan mail. That way we know if we've screwed up somewhere and/or done something that offends fans, or if we've done something wonderful that we should continue doing."

Klingons have been popular on STAR TREK—THE NEXT GENERATION and the fans wanted to know whatever happened to the two Klingon women, Lursa and Beitor?

"I love Klingons!" Frakes announced. "I like their food and women! Michael has done his Klingon thing now and is a lot more mellow than he used to be."

As though it just came to him, Frakes suddenly told an anecdote about himself in high school. "I'll tell you a story about my high school French teacher, Madame Maumbere, who is from this area. I was a prankster, terrorist and cut-up in her class. One day she had had it. She took me upstairs, looked at me and said, 'Jonathan, you should never have children!' I retorted, 'With you, Madame Maumbere?"

Riker plays poker in the show just as Frakes does in real life, and asked whether he plays well, Jonathan said, "I'd like to think so. But Ray Wise from DAYS OF OUR LIVES is a great poker player. I know from losing when that cast got together to play a few hands."

Asked what the most professionally challenging thing about playing Riker is, Frakes admitted, "Keeping it fresh and honest."

When someone wanted to know how Jonathan spends his free time, he replied, "What free time? Actually I play tennis with Michael Dorn. Wednesday nights I'm trombone jamming with a small group. I listen to jazz, read, and mostly I'm on a plane to New York every chance I get so I can be with my wife, Genie."

THIS REPORTER'S OPINION

Jonathan Frakes was in extremely high spirits for obvious reasons; his wife Genie Francis was with him that weekend, sitting in the audience. He spoke candidly but with diplomacy during both performances.

I admit being a skeptic at first, having watched his ARSENIO HALL appearance where Jonathan had outspokenly bashed Trekkies and STAR TREK conventions during Arsenio's interview. However, his open and humble apology to the convention audience for his remarks cleaned the slate for me. I hope he will continue to make that apology part of his "act" at future conventions until he has shared his repentant feelings with many more of his fans.

Music has always been a large part of the shared experience which is STAR TREK, and THE NEXT GENERATION is no exception.

Chapter Fourteen
THE MUSIC OF THE NEXT GENERATION

Music has long been an integral part of establishing the atmosphere of STAR TREK. In the '60s, Alexander Courage composed the now classic theme for the original series. Background music was also an integral part of Classic STAR TREK and a number of the best composers in television history worked on that series. This includes such names as Gerald Fried, Sol Kaplan, Jerry Fielding and Fred Steiner.

Mark Banning works for GNP Crescendo, the company which has has released three soundtracks featuring the music heard on episodes of STAR TREK—THE NEXT GENERATION. Mark has been the co-producer on that series of soundtrack albums and works with both the original composers as well as the studio in selecting the music cuts which are featured on the albums. Banning, and company president Neil Norman, have long been fans of the music heard in science fiction films.

While other companies over the years have released albums which present new versions of popular science fiction music, GNP presents only the original music heard in the films and television series.

"Everything we've done from STAR TREK has all been original recordings. In the case of the classic Trek soundtracks we've either used material belonging to the composer or tapes that have been salvaged by private collectors. We've used these as masters for production on albums like THE CAGE, WHERE NO MAN HAS GONE BEFORE, which was the first pilot soundtrack we did back in 1986."

BY JAMES VAN HISE

Said Banning, "We just recently did one with Dennis McCarthy from his scores for 'Yesterday's Enterprise,' 'Unification' and 'Hollow Pursuits.' It's an exceptional album in the fact that the 'Yesterday's Enterprise' score was nominated for an Emmy. And 'Unification' part one actually won the Emmy last year. So we've got a good double-clout on that album."

ORIGINAL MUSIC WEEK TO WEEK

Viewers and listeners who have been watching television for many years may not realize that the sound-tracks on TV shows have changed in the last decade or so. It was once commonplace for old TV shows, such as the original STAR TREK, to craft a number of interesting background melodies and then just re-edit and recycle them throughout various episodes. But this is no longer done on modern TV shows.

"There is always a new score for every episode shot," Mark explained. "There are certain passages which utilize a lot of the same themes and very much sound alike. But there's always been a brand new score for every episode. Tracking has been kept at an absolute minimum. It has only been done on a couple of shows in the earlier part of the year. Apart from that

they really try to avoid it whenever possible."

This is largely because of the changes in contracts with the musicians union over the years.

THE SEDATE STAR TREK UNIVERSE

"In the production of our albums, we have to find what episodes are remembered the best as well as how powerful their scores are," Banning stated, but finding the right music isn't as easy as one would think considering that there's more than 150 episodes to choose from.

Powerful scores have traditionally been very popular with science fiction film enthusiasts, but inexplicably the producers of STAR TREK—THE NEXT GENERATION don't like to use those types of musical scores on the show.

"Producers have clamped down a lot on the composer's creativity," Mark stated. "They don't get to use bombastic, melodic themes that jump out at you. You'd never get to hear anything like STAR WARS or INDIANA JONES on STAR TREK—THE NEXT GENERATION. The producers don't like the music to be that ostentatious. They prefer people listening to (the show's) technobabble and other things. Hopefully this year (season seven) we'll see a change."

The earlier seasons of NEXT GENERATION when Robert Justman was producer was much different in its approach to using different styles of music. "He liked music a lot. He encouraged a great deal to be as thematic and melodic as possible, which is more than evident in the classic series. The first couple of years of NEXT GEN were pretty much like that. Since he left and Rick Berman and Peter Lauritson took over, they were pretty much free to enforce their own views of the music, and that was simply that it not be overheard over the dialogue. As a result you have scores which are very ambient sounding. They're okay—it's not really bad music, but it's not really interesting music. A lot of it doesn't really work on its own. It wouldn't capture the listener's interest on an album for very long."

They find it very difficult to include material like that on a soundtrack album which is supposed to be designed to entertain a listener and hold up under repeated play. There have been such themes which have come up recently though, such as Jay Chattaway's for "The Inner Light." That theme was also heard in an episode called "Lessons" in season six, and the company has had

a lot of people inquiring about that piece of music.

THE MAIN COMPOSER

Regarding the number of different composers who have worked on NEXT GENERATION, Banning stated that, "In the beginning they primarily liked to work with two people. Dennis McCarthy has been working for STAR TREK—THE NEXT GENERATION and DEEP SPACE NINE pretty much since it all started."

McCarthy has merged the classic STAR TREK theme of Alexander Courage with the new STAR TREK theme established by Jerry Goldsmith in STAR TREK— THE MOTION PICTURE. McCarthy had previously composed science fiction theme music for the series "V" as well as for the Paramount series MacGYVER. Bob Justman and Rick Berman were familiar with McCarthy's work and after the composer submitted a sample music tape, he was hired on.

"Gene Roddenberry always loved the Jerry Goldsmith theme for STAR TREK—THE MOTION PICTURE," McCarthy explained in describing the origins of the NEXT GENERATION theme. "In talking with Rick Berman and Bob Justman, we all came to the idea, as a group, to try using the Alexander Courage theme to start it out with. So I went home and turned on the horn section of the synthesizers and tried to put it together. It seemed to really fit the show, with the visuals of the ship warping off into space!"

That theme can now be heard along with the music score of the 2-hour pilot, "Encounter At Farpoint," on a recently released soundtrack album.

THE FIRST SOUNDTRACK ALBUM

In discussing the creation of the first NEXT GENERATION soundtrack album, McCarthy said that "what happened with 'Farpoint' was that we had enough music from that one episode where we could go ahead and use the original soundtrack and create an album. It was quick. It only took us about two days to mix it.

"I loved 'Farpoint' because I just said, 'give me a tape, give me a studio and let's do it!' It was fun because when you do television, you can't spend three days doing one cue. You spend one day doing three shows!" laughs McCarthy. "You have the excitement of the immediate performance. A lot of the cuts on the soundtrack album were done in one take! Because of time, some of them were not even fully rehearsed!

There just isn't time in television to sit around and have coffee and talk. It's 'hit it boys, and you're dead!'"

So McCarthy is pleased at the outcome?

"It's got energy. It's got life. I hear myself talking in the background!" One of the unusual items contained in the album is an alternate theme never used in the show. It's one which had unpretentious beginnings.

"The alternate theme was only a rehearsal we happened to tape. It wasn't something planned. It was just, 'My gosh, we have 20 minutes! Let's just tape something here.' I wrote the theme for myself, for my internal use, to portray the Captain."

THE MUSIC OF DENNIS McCARTHY

McCarthy's name may not be familiar to devoted collectors of TV and movie soundtracks. That's because he's a relative newcomer to the business. Past work includes DYNASTY and in the mid-eighties the two hour premiere of the revival of POLICE STORY.

"I was a road musician for years. I started from the very beginning, as a pianist and a conductor," McCarthy stated. "I got into scoring accidentally. I never studied music. I just played the piano as a kid and I started getting work when I was at college, doing rock and roll things.

"I fell into music. While I was playing piano, I never knew how to read (sheet music). I finally had to at one point. It was, 'Okay, this is a C, this is a D,' and take it from there."

In the late 1970s, McCarthy's first score was completed in England for a film he refuses to name ("It was my first thing—I'm too embarrassed.") Upon returning to Los Angeles he showed it to the proper people in Warner Brothers and from there he's been working in the business ever since.

Many cast-members of the show have shown a genuine interest in the creation of the music for the series. Jonathan Frakes, who plays Commander William Riker, has stopped by recording sessions to watch and see how the post-production end of the show is assembled.

"Most of the performers have cassettes of the soundtrack and they like it and are excited about it," McCarthy revealed. "It's just a sort of family feeling on the show. Everybody works very hard. There's gripes and worries but we do get a great show going."

Sharp readers will note that Jonathan Frakes is something of a musician himself. In the first season's "11001001," he played the trombone in a holodeck sequence as the actor also plays the trombone in real life as well.

NEXT GENERATION: THE EARLY YEARS

"In the early years, Ron Jones worked with Dennis as his co-composer and they both had quite a distinctive style," Mark Banning continued. "Dennis liked a more on-going thematic movement with material he recreated for various episodes throughout. Ron Jones' style is more electronic, more synthetic. He liked to develop a thematic movement for each individual episode. He had his own theme for Romulans, Klingons, Tasha Yar or whoever. These were movements he reused any time these elements were present."

Towards the end of the third or fourth season, Ron Jones was let go because he was reluctant to follow the producers' wishes in doing more ambient, non-thematic scores. Then they brought in Jay Chattaway.

"He did a score for 'Tin Man' which was very nice; a very melodic piece until they told him, 'We don't want any of that. Tone it down.' Then in accordance with the producer's wishes, his next scores were more non-thematic and in the ambient vein that the producers wanted.

So they were happy with that and they kept him on after they let Ron Jones go."

There was a score in the first year of STAR TREK—THE NEXT GENERATION, in the third episode, "Code of Honor," which was done by Fred Steiner who did a lot of music for the old show. This music had an old show feel to it which apparently the producers didn't like because it struck them as too cliché, so they never used him again.

"Don Davis did an episode recently called 'Face of the Enemy,' which is a very nice piece. And they used John Debney on a couple of occasions; he's now scoring the new SEAQUEST series." But all in all it has largely been two people scoring the music for STAR TREK—THE NEXT GENERATION for most of the first six years and now on DEEP SPACE NINE.

SCORING AN EPISODE

The process of scoring an episode begins by giving the composer a copy of a rough cut of a show two weeks before the scoring date. They are also given a sheet directing exactly where in the story they want music to appear. The composer then goes over that and uses their own creativity to decide what would work best for that scene. They write it out and play it on their own synthesizer equipment and then bring it in for the orchestra to record about two weeks before the episode actually airs.

As to why the producers of STAR TREK—THE NEXT GENERATION object to the more bombastic film scores and want them toned down on the show, Banning admits, "This is something I've never really understood about their decisions. Basically, from all we've been able to gather, they feel that music distracts. They want people listening to the dialogue of the story; they don't want people listening to the music. They feel, for whatever reason, that music takes away from the visual as opposed to adding any kind of emotion, feeling or depth. None of us can understand their reasoning. A good score can add to what might otherwise might be a lackluster episode, but they just apparently don't seem to believe it. And anybody that tries to turn in a nice thematic, melodic piece would be sacked on the spot.

"It's like when Don Davis did 'Face of the Enemy' it was a nice melodic piece and was about the most in your face music that had appeared on STAR TREK for some time and the producers didn't like it. They won't hire him again. They prefer the music to be down there. They'd rather the people hear the sound effects and the dialogue. They prefer air conditioning noise over any nice melodic piece that might add a strong sense of emotion over action.' "

A MUSICAL CONTROVERSY

"I don't know if you read a recent CINEFANTASTIQUE article that was published. Basically it aired a lot of grievances, including my own, about what the music does and why it is the way it is and why we don't like it to be the way it is. And whereas the producers were not altogether appreciative of the fact that such an article was written, I think it might've opened their eyes a little bit to the fact that we need to rethink the music process. As I understand it, Rick Berman met with Dennis McCarthy in regards to the matter. I'm not sure exactly how it came out, but my knowledge is that Dennis will be given more creative control over how the music is done."

THE SOUNDTRACKS OF STAR TREK

The music for DEEP SPACE NINE has been relatively handcuffed, but not as bad. "We did an album of Dennis McCarthy's music

from the pilot episode of DEEP SPACE NINE and there he got to do a lot that he normally wouldn't get to do in STAR TREK at all. So that ended up being a really wonderful album. We even recorded a special version of it which we've marketed as a 'radio edit single,' which has gotten some highly recommended rotation on many adult contemporary radio stations. So we're doing very well with that and we certainly hope to do more."

The GNP Crescendo STAR TREK albums are available through many major record stores such as Warehouse and Tower. They also have a toll free number (1-800-654-7029) which people can use to order CD's and tapes or even to just request a current catalog. The records are also commonly sold at many major science fiction conventions around the country.

"Crescendo Records has been in business now for forty years," Mark revealed. "And we have some more good things happening in the future. Right now we're in the middle of producing an album on the QUANTUM LEAP television series. Like STAR TREK it has developed a great fan following and I think is destined for long future syndication as well as possible additional TV and/or feature films."

THE STORY BEHIND THE SOUNDS

When an original soundtrack is recorded in the United States, there is what is known as a reuse fee which means that the musicians who originally performed in the orchestra have to be paid again for the use of their music for commercial purposes. They're paid once for its use in the film, but if it gets put on a record then they have to get paid again, which can amount to thousands of dollars because if it's a 30 year old recording, the musicians have to be paid at modern scale rates, not 30 year old rates.

"In many cases, background score soundtracks do not have the major selling potential of rock compilation albums or vocal albums of any sort. And so largely the process is not really cost effective for many record companies. The film PREDATOR had a nice score by Alan Silvestri. It won awards but it had never been put out because it was recorded here in the states and the high reuse fees involved would never have been able to justify the production of an album. But if a score is recorded overseas in London or Munich, or even Moscow, the reuse fees don't apply, so it's easier to put out a soundtrack album in those cases and it's also easy to expand it and put down 60 or 70 minutes of music.

"Another restriction where the reuse fees are involved is that it has to be paid in increments of 15 minutes of music at a time. When you get over 45 minutes the cost really starts to go up, but usually if you keep it down to between 30 and 45, you can get away with a reasonably minimal cost of producing the album. But by and large, unless it really has some selling potential then it won't be bothered with at all. That's basically how the system works."

The music of STAR TREK—THE NEXT GENERATION is evidently continuing to grow and change as the producers realize that viewer expectations are much higher than they had previously thought. The music heard in "Descent" did show a slight change towards a more dramatic style although it is clearly nothing like the grand approach employed in the motion pictures. It makes one wonder what the style of music will be in the first NEXT GENERATION motion picture when it comes to the big screen in 1995.

They also serve who only stand and wait.

Chapter Fifteen

GUY VARDIMAN: STANDING IN FOR DATA

Guy Vardiman bounded up on the stage sporting a boyish grin and looking every bit the "model" of a STAR TREK—THE NEXT GENERATION off-duty male. Guy was wearing tight jeans, dark blue shirt and tan leather jacket. Quick with a joke, he explained that many people have never heard of him on the show because he's always in the background, the camera's focus, or being shown from the back. That's because he acts as a "double" or "stand-in" for Brent Spiner. Guy also performs his role as: Geordi's legs; Picard's, Data's and Riker's hands; Worf's shoulders, and for other males on the show as necessary when directors add the little details to shots in episode sequences.

At this convention in November 1991, Guy Vardiman performed his guest appearance speech for an hour. Later in the program he gave another one hour ST—TNG slide show (mostly 5th season shots with a few STAR TREK 6 shots), telling hilarious mini-stories about the filming of each scene. Guy opened his guest appearance by explaining that he has been working on the show as Brent Spiner's double since the 10th episode of the first season.

Regarding whether he was also involved in being the stunt-double for Brent Spiner, Vardiman explained, "No, I'm not a stunt double. Another cast member performs Mr. Spiner's stunts, even minor ones requiring weight to be carried as Brent has a bad back. For example, in the opening scene of 'Silicon Avatar,' Data has to carry a child across a field to run from the crystal entity. Brent had to

Is it live or is it Memorex? Brent Spiner with Marina Sirtis at the Project Robin Hood food drive for L.I.F.E.

Photo © 1993 Albert L. Ortega

do one take as Mr. Spiner hurt his back performing it."

A STAR TREK CONSULTANT

Guy has also performed in other capacities for THE NEXT GENERATION.

"Another job I had done for the past couple of seasons is to assist Richard Arnold, STAR TREK Research Consultant in the STAR TREK Office. The STAR TREK Office handles fan mail, researches and reviewes scripts for consistency to the STAR TREK universe and continuity of events just before filming. He also assisted STAR TREK and STAR TREK—THE NEXT GENERATION stars with convention appearances, etc. One of my last and favorite projects with the STAR TREK Office was the

film that scene because his face would be prominent throughout the shot. Unfortunately they could only organizing, coordinating and arranging of the many STAR TREK props and articles donated for the 25th

TREK exhibit at the Smithsonian Institute, in Washington, D.C."

That was his last project because a week before, shortly after Gene Roddenberry's death, Richard Arnold and Guy Vardiman were "let go" and the STAR TREK Office has been disbanded.

"After Gene Roddenberry's death, Paramount executives decided to cut the studio budget by doing away with that function inside Paramount. So they have hired a less expensive outside consulting firm, DeForest Research, to perform our jobs. I feel very fortunate to remain employed in my stand-in job with STAR TREK—THE NEXT GENERATION," Vardiman observed.

THE STAR TREK MOTION PICTURES

He also said that he was honored to be performing as a STAR TREK actor in his third job—he'd been selected to be an extra in the cast of STAR TREK VI—THE UNDISCOVERED COUNTRY. Guy laughed about being, once again, an unrecognizable figure. He revealed that he and Production Associate Eric Stillwell were chosen to play Klingon characters. Guy lamented, though, that their roles called for Guy and Eric to be perched way, way, wayyyy up in the top of the Klingon-filled stadium in the Kirk and McCoy trial scene.

Vardiman joked about being so far from the cameras that the make-up artists didn't need to apply Klingon makeup and turtlehead appliances. Instead the clandestine STAR TREK—THE NEXT GENERATION members wore smotheringly hot, slip-on masks, plus weighty sweat-producing uniforms at an un-air conditioned pinnacle height of the stage set. They also had to hold perfectly still most of the time during the filming. Being true blue STAR TREK fans since they were youngsters, Guy and Eric stuck it out, literally.

Guy was asked how different any STAR TREK—THE NEXT GENERATION movies would be from the past STAR TREK motion pictures?

"In the STAR TREK movies that producer Harve Bennett was involved, Harve believed in, and created, the far more militaristic STAR TREK plots. However, when the STAR TREK movies were being made, Gene Roddenberry wanted them to have a more peaceful STAR TREK—THE NEXT GENERATION appearance. Hopefully, with Gene gone, the STAR TREK—THE NEXT GENERATION movies will still accomplish Gene's goal."

CONTINUITY GLITCHES

Since he had worked as a researcher, Guy was asked what sort of continuity problems and inconsistencies he'd found on the show?

"There have been many inconsistencies in past STAR TREK— THE NEXT GENERATION episodes," he explained. "Remember when Data had super-speed and strength? For example, during 'Identity Crisis,' when the film crew was lining up the shot where Geordi tries to join the slowly wobbling lizard people? Well, Brent argued for half an hour that Data should have been able to run and catch the creatures easily. In another scene when the Away Team runs towards a cave? Data's speed should have allowed him to reach there well ahead of the rest of the crew!

"During earlier seasons, writers created humorous scenes that compared Data's unusual strength and speed to the outmatched crew's. In the cave scene, they missed an opportunity to add a moment of comedy. The scene could have shown Data leisurely leaning against the cave entrance, appearing rested and bored, as the Away Team sprints up to Data, out of breath. If episodes break with continuity, the writers should come up with reasons to justify Data's non-use of his android talents, like Data had to excuse himself and beam up to get his tricorder or something."

Regarding what the hardest part of the job was for the actors, Guy stated, "For Brent it's the technobabble. When cast members forget their lines, or a director requires the same scenes to be filmed from many angles, or something on the set messes up, Brent has to keep saying the same long lines again and again. Frequently the cast is required to repeat the scene's dialogue 20 to 30 times.

"For Worf the problem of saying technobabble is compounded by the fact that he has to wear false teeth over his real ones. It's difficult for him to enunciate some of the words clearly during filming. Mike Okuda and Rick Sternbach are the production's technical advisors. They work very hard to insure that the sci-fi technical aspects of the dialogue are as scientifically accurate or at least fictionally well constructed as possible."

As to how many fan written scripts make it as episodes per season, Guy said, "Only about two to three out of twenty-six each season. They have a whole mountain of scripts stacked in a large room. They're sent to Paramount from all over the world, both with and without agents' support."

HUMOR AND HEARTACHE

So what is it like to work with Whoopi Goldberg?

"It's a hoot! She is so funny! I have to tell you a story about Whoopi. Once when Whoopi was on Arsenio Hall's show, Arsenio asked her why all the black people on STAR TREK—THE NEXT GENERATION have something funny wrong with them (such as Geordi LaForge's VISOR) or something different about them (like Worf's turtlehead and Guinan's strange costumes and mystical powers). Whoopi explained that Worf was a Klingon and no one can tell he's actually black because of his make-up and appliances. Also there are guest stars and minor crew members that don't look any different than the other actors."

Vardiman mentioned that something unusual happened when he was filming the "Brothers" episode—he got into a car accident before he was supposed to perform as a stand-in for the characters of Dr. Soong, Lore and Data.

"The accident was serious enough that I was out of work for four months. So I missed seeing exactly how the production staff created Data's twin effects. I know that Brent had to play all three roles while timing each character's action synchronously to correspond to the other character's movements without having the benefit of a person being there during filming. Then Brent had to play the opposite character in the scene and remember precisely when to make a reciprocating movement. But I did get to work on 'Datalore.'

VARDIMAN'S FINAL STORY

"I have an idea for a STAR TREK—THE NEXT GENERATION movie," he suggested, although his idea was for a movie to take place immediately following the sixth season of the series, which at one point was thought to be the probable end of the show's run. "Remember during the 'Brothers' episode when Lore explains to Data and Dr. Soong that he didn't get destroyed after Wesley Crusher beamed him into space? Then Lore drifted in space for two years until a Pakled ship finds him? Finally Lore steals the emotions chip meant for Data, presses the transporter button in his finger and beams back to his ship? Well imagine a plot where Lore's next move upon his return is to become king of the Pakleds! Then dressed in Data's uniform, Lore begins a rampage of terror across the galaxy. The STAR TREK—THE NEXT GENERATION movie mission of the U.S.S. Enterprise is to stop Lore before he destroys the entire Federation! There's no doubt in my mind that Brent would enjoy playing a psycho-chip-gone-bad-android!"

Interesting how close that plot idea was to what viewers saw presented in the multi-part adventure "Descent" in the sixth and seventh seasons of STAR TREK—THE NEXT GENERATION.

As usual, the sixth season of THE NEXT GENERATION featured high-quality effects of the level fans have come to expect over the years. Work continues at the Culver City site of Digital Magic, where the latest developments in video effects are brought to bear with relentless intensity on the adventures of Jean-Luc Picard and his stalwart crew. There are, as always, two teams of special effects masters working on the show under the watchful eye of the special effects producer, Dan Curry.

One such team is headed by visual effects supervisor Ron Moore and his assistant Phil Barberioo; the other is led by David Stipes and David Takemura. Eddie Williams, a visual effects associate, works with both teams to assure consistency. Together, these men and their associ-

Chapter Sixteen

FUTURE EFFECTS: RECENT ADVANCES ON THE NEXT GENERATION

ates are the ones who really bring the visuals of THE NEXT GENERATION to life.

One of the challenges facing this brilliant team during the sixth season was the creation, or re-creation, of the classic Enterprise bridge for the Scotty resurrection episode, "Relics." A holodeck scene in which Scotty revisits the bridge of his old ship was originally cut from the script when the cost of rebuilding a complete set from scratch proved to be too expensive. The scene was revived when it became obvious that this was a critical scene for that episode; as long as it could be done in a cost-effective manner, it stayed in.

Richard James, a production designer for the show, realized that the key to the problem lay in locating a shot from the original STAR TREK that showed the bridge with no one on the set. In time, one was located, a few brief seconds from "This Side Of Paradise" which shows James Kirk leaving the bridge of his abandoned ship. The tail end of this scene had just enough footage to create a stock background shot through extensive duplication and looping. Then, a sliver of the set was built using photos as reference, as no original blueprints exist.

This fragment, including the captain's chair, was used against a blue-screen, enabling James Doohan and Patrick Stewart to appear to walk through the old set to the central bridge area. There, on the physical set, their scene was shot. The backdrop to Stewart's shots were moved and re-dressed to do double duty as the background to Doohan's shots. The real coup in this brilliant but affordable set-up: a captain's chair and helm built by a diehard TREK fan some years earlier for his detailed, home-made set replica, most of which no longer exists. The final detail: console buttons from the classic STAR TREK, given to miniature expert Greg Jein by the original series' effects supervisor Jimmy Rugg and lent to THE NEXT GENERATION by Jein.

SPECIAL CHALLENGES

One reason for all these budgetary constraints in "Relics" was the other main effects problem for the episode: how to construct a full-fledged Dyson Sphere and remain in the black? Originally, Digital Computer Imaging was considered, but this would actually have been more expensive than the old, tried-and-true method which was finally utilized: miniature models. Greg Jein designed and built the panels of the Dyson Sphere (an immense construction that encloses an entire solar system), which were then duplicated digitally to create the illusion of the artifact's overwhelming size.

On a human level, THE NEXT GENERATION used the technology developed for such films as David Cronenberg's DEAD RINGERS to create the illusion of two Rikers on the screen at one time in the episode "Second Chances." Computer camera control allowed them to keep the camera moving in the scenes, avoiding the static shots that have long been the bane of such split-screen scenes ever since the dawn of cinema. Gone, too, is the telltale vertical line that for so many years had to be strategically placed in the background or foreground to mask the line of demarcation between the two elements of the scene.

MAKE-UP AND OTHER EFFECTS

On the make-up front, monster master Michael Westmore continued to create the widely varied background array of aliens for both THE NEXT GENERATION and DEEP SPACE NINE. His make-up jobs have become more detailed than ever, using sculpting rather than just paint to create appliances and effects that vary in appearance according to the lighting. With a higher budget than ever before, he nonetheless economizes, using aliens in the background in one show and bringing them forward as featured characters in the other. Case in point: Shrek, the alien who feeds Worf false information about his father in the two-part NEXT GENERATION episode "Birthright."

Acute observers of both shows might have noticed Shrek hanging out in the Promenade on DEEP SPACE NINE for several episodes before THE NEXT GENERATION aired "Birthright." A busy man, Westmore has also created the heads for the mannequins of NEXT GENERATION/DS9 characters that will appear in a display scheduled to appear in Paramount-owned amusement parks around the country.

An unusually high quotient of digital graphics effects were used in the episode "Frame Of Mind," in which Riker, a prisoner of mysterious aliens, is place in their equivalent of a repressive mental hospital. But his "treatment" as such is that he is made to believe that he is in a play on board the Enterprise, directed by Beverly Crusher, in which he is playing a prisoner struggling to retain his dignity and identity. As the ever shifting reality changes again and again, Riker is forced to doubt both his sanity, and the reality of everything around him. When his performance in the "play" is wildly applauded by a strangely alien version of the Enterprise crew, Riker shoots himself with his own phaser. The result is a spectacular CGI (Computer-Generated Imagery) shot in which Riker's apparent reality shatters like a mirror into countless shards, revealing another reality underneath.

On a more mundane level, "Frame Of Mind" also included a scene in which Dr. Crusher treats Riker for a minor injury. Crusher points a medical device at a bleeding wound on Riker's face, and its glowing red tip heals the wound. The wound was created with make-up, and the device was a simple prop; the rest was done with computers by Steve Scott. The computer in question is known as Harry; it is operated by "drawing" with a pen on a special pad, enabling operators much more artistic leeway than a mouse or a trackball. This effects shot was quite a simple affair with this technology in hand.

First up was the simple task of removing the wound about halfway through the sequence. Then, backing up a bit, a red glow was painted in such a manner as to make it look as if it were coming from somewhere within Crusher's device. The final component: a focused red spot on Riker's face. This all takes just a few seconds of screen time, but it looks absolutely convincing, despite the amazing simplicity of its execution!

SPECIAL MISTAKES

Sometimes glitches in production are removed; sometimes they are not. The next time "Unification II" is shown in syndication, videotape it and play back, in slow motion, the scene where Data KOs a Romulan with a Vulcan neck pinch: a sound man is clearly visible, reflected in the base of a lamp! In this season's "Lessons," all window backgrounds during a warp-speed sequence showed the familiar blurred-starfield effect— except the window in Picard's office, which showed the stars outside in their usual still configuration.

Another long-standing problem along these lines was finally eradicated during the sixth season. For quite some time, phaser props had a small light inside them, activated when the actors pulled the trigger— but the actors almost always pulled the trigger as they drew their phasers, which obliged the effects crew to remove the light anyway. Finally, by removing the batteries from the props, the problem was eradicated, and all phaser effects, even the light inside them, is done optically rather than live.

Ultimately, the best effects are frequently accomplished by the most simple means. When Riker was "floated" out of his quarters by alien abductors in "Schism" (Riker had this problem a lot this season, it seems) Dan Curry pulled of a shot without wires by shooting sideways a sequence of a stunt man falling. Simply by turning the shot back sideways and slowing it down considerably, Curry produced a usable effect with no visible means of support. It is this kind of basic problem-solving thinking, as much or more than the expensive special effects equipment at their disposal, that makes the effects experts for STAR TREK—THE NEXT GENERATION to consummate wizards they truly are.

Collector, special effects creator, model builder and current owner of one of three original Captain's chairs, he's parlayed his hobby into creatively contributing to STAR TREK—THE NEXT GENERATION.

Chapter Seventeen
PROPS TO THE STARS

When the script calls for a certain well known British Secret Service Agent to fall into a pit teaming with hungry maggots, who do you call to conjure up the squirmy little devils and still have your actor available for your next movie?-Greg Stone.

When the bodies of certain Starfleet officers are inhabited by a parasitical being who scurries around on six legs, is six inches long, and has long protruding mandibles, who do you call to manufacture, articulate and deliver these beasties all within nine days of the episode going on the air?-Greg Stone.

Greg Stone is fast becoming a rising star in the cosmos of special effects creations. To date he has done independent special effects work for the latest James Bond movie,

LICENSE TO KILL, and the "Conspiracy" episode for STAR TREK—THE NEXT GENERATION. Greg, who works full time for a collections agency in Los Angeles, first acquired his taste for science fiction back when the original STAR TREK episodes were first being shown. After the show went off the air, he continued to cultivate his interest over the years, growing more and more fascinated by the special effects end of it.

EXPLOSIVE CONTACT WITH STAR TREK

In 1975/76 he was called upon to help Bjo Trimble with the construction of a bridge set which was going to be shown at a STAR TREK convention. It was at this convention (more specifically known as Equicon) that Greg met Ralph Miller. Ralph shared a similar interest in

STAR TREK and special effects work. Together they teamed up to learn all they could about the subject. Eventually this led them into the special effects, model making end of their hobby. Together they created the special effects, model making company which has done the aforementioned work for the two movies.

For the Trek episode "Conspiracy," Greg, with the help of his friend David Stipes, built 20 articulated parasite creatures and 50 non-articulated ones out of a special kind of foam rubber at David's studio in Los Angeles. The original design of the creature was done by Andrew Probert, Senior Graphic Illustrator for the first season of STAR TREK—THE NEXT GENERATION. Greg got the job assignment through a friend at a local special effects shop who told him that a specific creature was needed to be built for an episode of ST—TNG. Taking a week off from his job in Santa Ana, he put together the effect which was called to be in the film in 9 days! Not only was he able to pull it off in the short time he was given, but it was one of the more popular episodes of the first season.

A FAN AND COLLECTOR

Greg is also a collector of STAR TREK memorabilia. The pride and joy of his collection is one of three original Captain's chairs from the original series which he acquired fifteen years ago. It sits in the corner of his living room rightfully adorned by STAR TREK posters on the wall behind it. Also in his collection are two of the original swivel chairs usually seen on the bridge, briefing room, or guest quarters. These seats, seen throughout the ship in the original series, were designed and built at the Brunswick company, the same company who makes seats and lanes for bowling alleys throughout America.

The chairs were custom made for the series with the incorporation of the swivel which, no matter where it was pointed, would always come back to the front. These chairs also had removable padded vinyl backs which slipped on and off the tops of the chairs. They also had vinyl cushions which were slipped on and off when the occasion called for it. After the show's demise, these chairs could be seen in Mrs. Brady's kitchen on the TV show THE BRADY BUNCH.

The history of the Captain's chair, however, is a little darker. There were three chairs built during the entire production of the original series. The first chair is the one seen on the original pilot of "The Cage." As the story goes, when production of "The Cage" was completed, the sets went into storage. Later, when a second pilot was ordered ("Where No Man Has Gone Before") they were without a chair. It was gone. So another had to be constructed. This one lasted through STAR TREK's first and second seasons. According to Greg, the difference in both chairs can be noticed in the wooden arms rests on the inside of the chair, and in the color and angle of the armrest.

The final chair was made for the production of the third season. The first and second season chair had been used, twisted, turned, and sat in so much that it was showing signs of wear and tear. It is this third season chair that Greg has acquired. How he acquired it is an interesting story.

A UNIQUE COLLECTIBLE

When the show was canceled in 1968, the prop was acquired from Paramount by a party (who shall remain nameless) who moved to Ohio. Greg bought the chair from this person in Ohio years ago at the hefty sum of $750.00 The previous owner had placed the chair out in his garage (after the initial charm of having it faded for him) where it consequently found its way out to the yard. Uncovered and unprotected the weather took its toll on the chair.

When Greg acquired it, the chair had no black vinyl seat in it. All he had were the base, the side panels, and a hole where the seat should have been. The color of the wood, which was actually part wood and part fiberboard, had gone from a flat white on the TV show to a moldy dark color. Black and splotchy areas covered the chair. The particle board had deteriorated and the control boards located on either arm rests were gutted. All the circuitry had been pulled out. The chair was soft in places where water had gotten into the wood. Greg and his partner set out to restore the chair.

Armed with fiberglass, and additional fiberboard and resin, it took them over 300 man hours over the course of 11 months to restore the chair to its almost original form. They acquired some padding, covered it with black vinyl and made a new seat to fill the hole. So now one could sit in the chair. The panels were replaced, all in the right order and color scheme but no new wiring was put in. No lights flash when you push the buttons on the arm of the chair.

They have displayed the fruits of their combined labor only at two conventions so far. Once at the 20th anniversary convention in 1986 at Disneyland, and again at a convention mot long after that where William Shatner attended as a guest speaker. Shatner had reportedly seen the chair there and had sat in it, commenting that "it still felt good after all this time."

LOOKING TO THE FUTURE

Eventually Greg and Ralph would like to see their restoration efforts reflected on the big screen in a future STAR TREK story involving the original sets. They also wish to continue collecting memorabilia wherever and whenever they can find it. Greg and his partner assisted in assembling the sound effects for the music tape done by Crescendo Records of "The Cage" and "Where No Man Has Gone Before." Ralph's name appears on the credits of the sound effects tape.

Both these men learned their complicated craft the hard way—by trial and error. Learning from people in the business. Making their own molds and using their own materials. Greg started 15 years ago by taking classes in graphic arts, and he said, "it helps to have an eye for blueprint detail." He improved his talents by learning foam latex appliance techniques and armature construction in the use of model building from some friends in the business.

In all Greg Stone and Ralph Miller are two of the most dedicated people in the special effects field.

And if the seriousness, attention to detail, and devotion to craft is any indication of their love affair with science fiction, the props they help restore may very well find themselves lasting way into the 23rd century.

By now the word is out: the seventh season of STAR TREK—THE NEXT GENERATION may well be its last, as preparations get underway for the long-expected move of the Enterprise-D and crew to the big screen. Without a crystal ball however,

Chapter Eighteen

NEWS FROM THE FRONT: THE PENULTIMATE SEASON

there is no way to see what that particular future holds (although there are already rumors that TNG will continue into an eighth season after all). But plenty happened behind the scenes during the sixth season, which is well worth examining in detail.

This season marked Michael Piller's third year with THE NEXT GENERATION, both as executive producer and head writer. It also marked his move over to the new companion series, STAR TREK—DEEP SPACE NINE, which premiered halfway through THE NEXT

GENERATION's regular season. Despite this, Piller managed to keep a hand in with THE NEXT GENERATION. But he sees the seventh year of THE NEXT GENERATION as his last. Even if the show comes back for an eighth year, Piller will be elsewhere seeking new ground.

The sixth season was a hectic one, with staff exodus to DEEP SPACE NINE, tighter production schedules than usual, and an unfortunate shortage of usable scripts which resulted in the widely varying quality of the series from episode to episode. Keeping all the scripts in development was Jeri Taylor, executive producer after Michael Piller and Rick Berman. Their new focus on DEEP SPACE NINE made Taylor's responsibilities on THE NEXT GENERATION all the more demanding, but

Taylor pulled it off with great aplomb. Taylor made it her mission, this past season, to reinforce the focus on the female characters, Deanna Troi and Beverly Crusher.

Taylor also fought to get her vision of Kehless to come across in "Rightful Heir." Winrich Kolbe, the director of that episode, wanted the legendary Klingon warrior to be a young, handsome and charismatic figure. Taylor saw him as older and wiser, although no less charismatic, and even made sure that he was shown to be much shorter than the average Klingon of the 24th Century, a nod to Napoleon Bonaparte. And it was through Taylor that many of the sixth season's finest episodes made their respective ways to the television screens of America.

LABORING BEHIND THE SCENES

Also sticking around were two of the most important NEXT GENERATION scripters: Brannon Braga and Ronald D. Moore. Braga, whose NEXT GENERATION debut "Reunion" saw the death of Worf's gal K'Ehleyr, provided such sixth season winners as "Frame of Mind," "Timescape," and "Schisms," as well as such less inspired fare as "Aquiel," the Barclay outing "Realm Of Fear," and half of the profoundly silly

"Fistful Of Datas." He also contributed the first part of "Birthright."

Ron Moore, the man behind most of the great Klingon episodes, created "Tapestry," and the first half of "Chain of Command" as well as the Scotty resurrection episode "Relics," and crafted the season finale, "Descent," as well. Another familiar name, Rene Echevarria, scripted "True Q" (featuring—guess who) and "Ship In A Bottle," which revived the Moriarty holodeck character with interesting results.

NEXT GENERATION science consultant Naren Shankar stepped into the writing foray with the exo-comp episode, "Quality of Life," and scripted "Face Of The Enemy" from a story by Rene Echevarria.

TROI: BACK IN STRIDE

Jeri Taylor's efforts to reinforce the female characters on STAR TREK—THE NEXT GENERATION certainly paid off as far as Marina Sirtis was concerned. Deanna Troi had plenty of screen time during the sixth season. And even though "A Fistful Of Datas" was the height of silliness, it did give Troi a break from the usual grind of being the ship's Counselor. Sirtis was pleased when the obtuse Captain Jellico (Ronnie Cox) told Deanna to wear her standard Starfleet uniform in "Chain of Command." Why would a uniform show so much cleavage, anyway?

Her character has worn a standard uniform on-duty ever since, although off-duty would seem to be a different matter, particularly in "Man Of The People," in which Deanna wore some truly revealing outfits and tossed sex appeal around like it was going out of style. And of course, in that episode, it was: soon enough, Deanna became a hideous old hag with a decidedly wicked temper. This was all very well and good as far as Marina Sirtis was concerned. Although she doesn't mind Deanna being sexy, she likes to have the chance to do more with the character than just that.

"Face Of The Enemy," in which she is abducted and transformed to look like a Romulan— an imposture that her life depends on— gave Sirtis plenty of room to stretch as an actress, and stands as one of her favorite episodes of all time. It was also one of the top-rated episodes of the sixth season!

Doctor Beverly Crusher did not get quite as much of the limelight as Counselor Troi, but she did get one star outing during the sixth season: "Suspicions" featured Gates McFadden's character in an unusual murder mystery. Even though this

was basically QUINCY in space, McFadden did a great job.

CHAIN OF COMMAND

"Chain of Command" was a harrowing two-part episode in which Captain Picard was captured and tortured by Cardassians while his replacement on the Enterprise, the unpleasant Captain Jellico, almost steers the ship on a course straight towards certain destruction. At first, "Chain Of Command" had been planned as the first crossover between THE NEXT GENERATION and DEEP SPACE NINE, but Rick Berman decided against it. Even so, the episode was aired in such a fashion as to lead, indirectly, to the debut of DEEP SPACE NINE, with is denouement essentially brought about by the easing of Federation/Starfleet tensions that made the events of the DEEP SPACE NINE premiere possible.

Originally a one-part episode, "Chain of Command" actually saved budget funds for THE NEXT GENERATION when it was expanded to two parts. The scenes in which Gul Madred (David Warner) tortured Picard were, essentially, a "bottle show," a one-room, two-actor set piece which saved money to be used in another episode. (Jellico's final confrontation with the Cardassians, it should be noted, also took place largely off screen, with no spectacular scenes of Cardassian ships facing the Enterprise in space.)

Once it was decided to expand that aspect of the storyline, Michael Piller came up with the simple but brilliant notion of contacting Amnesty International, the organization that draws attention to human rights abuses around the world, and which documents repression, political prisoners, abductions and torture in an effort to force governments to abandon these heavy handed tactics.

Patrick Stewart and Jeri Taylor had long been supporters of Amnesty International. In fact, to prepare for his performance in this episode, Patrick Stewart listened to audio tapes, provided by Amnesty International, of actual torture sessions.

Another influence on "Chain of Command" was a recent, but little-seen, movie entitled CLOSET LAND. This, too, was a two-character drama, in which Madeline Stowe played a political prisoner tortured by Alan Rickman. Early scripts for "Chain of Command" were considerably more graphic than the one filmed. Jeri Taylor did some anonymous rewriting which lessened the physicality of the torture while retaining its psychological violence.

And it was a success: despite the relative clumsiness of the Picard-turns-spy plot that sets up the story in the first half, the second half of "Chain of Command," with its interplay between David Warner and Patrick Stewart, really paid off.

Q REDUX

As if to make up for the absence of Q during the fifth season of STAR TREK—THE NEXT GENERATION, the show provided, not one, but two Q episodes. Q's absence the previous year had nothing to do with deLancie, however; two troublesome Q script ideas got bogged down in the mud of development during season five, and ultimately sank without a trace.

One of these, "Q Makes Two," would have posed serious logistical problems even if the script had been hammered into some sort of shape: the basic premise of "Q Makes Two" would have involved the creation, by Q, of an exact replica of the Enterprise and all of its crew, all in response to Picard's belief that humanity has shed all of its darker aspects. "Q Makes Two" would have been the ultimate evil twin episode (perhaps killing the idea for all television shows hence), "The Enemy Within" writ extra large, with the split crew learning, like James Kirk so many years before, that the two divided aspects of humanity cannot survive without each other.

Brannon Braga had hoped to have a scene in which the two Enterprises exchange fire, but the writing problems posed by doubling the regular characters and changing them appropriately for the situation was more than enough to sink "Q Makes Two" without even thinking about the budgetary restraints. Another Q script idea, "Q-Olympics," (which sounds potentially awful, even from the title!) met with a similarly dismal fate.

SON OF Q?

Oddly enough, Q's return finally came about in a script which was derived from a submission by a highschool student who came up with a scenario in which a young character discovers that he was actually a member of the Q Continuum. This Mary-Sue premise was reworked until it became "True Q." The closet Q in question became a young woman.

The character of Q has taken on considerably darker aspects in his more recent appearances, giving deLancie considerably more range for his talents: in "True Q," he is presented as being quite capable of killing Olivia D'Abo's character—

and in his next appearance he appears in Picard's near-death experience, claiming to be God!

"Tapestry" was sort of Jean-Luc Picard's IT'S A WONDERFUL LIFE. The first version of this episode owed a bit more to Charles Dickens. In fact, it was called "A Q Carol." In this draft, Q showed Picard a number of scenes from his past; in the final version, the story concentrated on one single, pivotal episode in Picard's life, a violent confrontation in which he was so seriously wounded that he had to have his original heart replaced with an artificial one. In the original version of "Tapestry," the storyline was a bit too busy to suit producer Michael Piller, so scripter Ron Moore headed back to his writing table and reworked the entire premise.

Lost in the rewrite were a number of potentially intriguing scenes: Picard as a child in France (portrayed by David Tristan Birkin from "Rascals," no doubt) growing up with his parents, and scenes on the Stargazer with Jack Crusher still alive, a chance to really learn something about this character who is largely an enigma. But all these details did not add up to a dramatically driven script. By focusing matters on the fateful bar fight, Moore created a truly compelling look at the past of THE NEXT GENERATION's key player.

24TH CENTURY CAMEOS

STAR TREK—THE NEXT GENERATION saw numerous visits by celebrities to the set. But more interesting and close to the heart of THE NEXT GENERATION, were two cameo appearances in different sixth-season episodes. In the episode "Second Chances" (the double Riker episode), NASA astronaut Mae Gremison appeared as a transporter operator (although not the one responsible for that episode's perplexing problem). And in the season cliffhanger "Descent," noted physicist Stephen Hawking played a holodeck representation of himself. The scene is amusing, a light prelude to the dark events of that episode: Data is on the holodeck playing poker with Hawking, Albert Einstein and Sir Isaac Newton. Hawking is the mathematics professor at Cambridge University (Newton's old job!), a brilliant scientist who has thrown the validity of the big bang theory into question with his work on black holes.

A controversial but highly respected figure, Hawking contacted Rick Berman while promoting the movie version of his book A BRIEF HISTORY OF TIME. An impromptu tour of the set of THE NEXT GENERATION led to the cameo appearance, with a little help from Leonard Nimoy, who had met Hawking at a party and learned of his desire to be on the show. Hawking cuts a unique figure: physically encumbered by Lou Gehrig's disease, he is wheelchair bound; unable to speak, he uses a computer-generated voice to talk, punching up words and phrases on a special thumb-operated keyboard.

Despite this vocal limitation, Hawking conveys a great deal of humor in his brief NEXT GENERATION appearance, rising above the bickering between Einstein and Newton (BARON MUNCHAUSEN's John Neville) to win big poker stakes, much to Data's bemusement. Brent Spiner contends that Hawking is a great actor: the scientist betrayed no nervousness at all on the set, while the actor was fairly intimidated by working with this indisputable genius!

DIRECTING THE ENTERPRISE

The sixth season of THE NEXT GENERATION also saw the usual roster of directors, including Cliff Bole, Les Landau, Winrich Kolbe, and Alexander Singer. Patrick

Stewart returned to the directorial chair with "A Fistful Of Datas," yet another poor choice but one which he pulled off fairly well despite the silly script. Jonathan Frakes fared somewhat better with "Quality Of Life."

It seems interesting that both actors directed episodes featuring Data— perhaps they realized that Brent Spiner was one fellow actor who would not let them down. Special effects maven Dan Curry directed "Birthright, Part Two," and did a commendable first-time job with this tale of Worf on his own. Jonathan Frakes came off a great deal better as the director of a superior episode, "The Chase," which introduced— briefly, as it turns out— Captain Picard's former archaeology professor.

But perhaps the most gratifying surprise in this field was LeVar Burton's directorial debut: "Second Chances," which pitted Will Riker against himself in a contest for Deanna Troi's affections. Adam Nimoy directed "Rascals" and "Timescape," faring much better with the second one due to a superior script. There was definitely no shortage of directorial talent during this past season.

BIRTHRIGHT

"Birthright" was first conceived as a straight-ahead story about Worf seeking his father in a Romulan prison camp, but was expanded into two episodes for several reasons. The first, obviously, was to explore more deeply the drama Worf is drawn into. The other reason was to save money by using the same sets for two episodes— a ploy which had been a rousing success for "Chain of Command," but one which, ironically, didn't work for "Birthright."

But the expansion of this tale yielded a true bonus in the subplot (in the first half only) of the birth of Data's ability to dream, one more step in the redoubtable android's ongoing quest to achieve true humanity. The idea originally emerged from Ron Moore's suggestion that Data might have a religious experience. The religious idea was toned down, but the result, involving the father-figure of Dr. Noonian Soongh (seen here as a young man) tied in nicely with the main theme of Worf's own father-quest.

(A side note here: back when Data was first discovered by Starfleet personnel, why didn't anyone notice the amazing resemblance between this remarkable android and Dr. Soongh? Since Soongh was a famous scientist of interstellar repute, who gave his own face to his two cybernetic humanoid creations, it seems likely that someone might have made the connection between Data and Soongh long before the events of "Datalore.") The dream sequence was basically a result of the need to avoid anything too similar to Picard's experiences in "Tapestry," as well.

A TALE OF KLINGONS AND ROMULANS

The plot involving Worf developed more strongly as a result of the expansion, also. Rather than standing merely as yet another fast-paced action adventure laden with Klingon-versus-Romulan action, "Birthright" was able to unfold at a pace which allowed the writers to examine the philosophical questions raised by having Klingons and Romulans living together in such close proximity for so many years.

On the special effects front, the prison camp as seen in long shots was created by employing photographs of Laotian jungles as the basis for matte shots. This was made all the more easy by the fact that director Dan Curry had toured Southeast Asia as a photographer years earlier, and had plenty of suitable photographs on hand in his personal files.

Despite the expansion, the second part of "Birthright" wound up being about a quarter of an hour too long, and scenes were cut which would have explained why the alien Shrek had sent Worf to the prison planet in the first place. The actor playing Shrek broke his leg during filming and was therefore out of the picture later in the shoot. Scenes that explained Shrek's own prison experiences with the Romulans were never filmed. Neither was the death of Shrek.

Apparently, Shrek will tell any Klingon a variation of what he told Worf, but was to have been killed by another Klingon who took the idea that his father had been taken prisoner as a personal affront to himself and his family! Strangely enough, the extra time only served to muddle up the conclusion of the Worf plotline— but the scenes of Data's dreaming in Part One will always stand as one of the key sequences in NEXT GENERATION history.

TO THE SILVER SCREEN

It's no secret: the production schedule for the seventh season of STAR TREK—THE NEXT GENERATION started a month earlier than usual. The reason? To have cast and crew ready to start filming the first NEXT GENERATION motion picture in April, 1994. Heading this campaign of creative media-hopping is none other than THE NEXT GENERATION's long-time head honcho, Rick Berman (who looks remarkably like SATURDAY NIGHT LIVE producer Lorne Michaels). After the success of THE NEXT GENERATION and its fledgling spin-off, DEEP SPACE NINE, Paramount was more than willing and ready to entrust Berman with the development and execution of the first big-screen adventure of Picard and his crew—which they hope to release regularly every two years.

The crucial factor in any NEXT GENERATION movie is, of course, the story. Paramount encouraged Berman to set up the development of three scripts. Berman opted to commission only two, and chose writers who not only have television experience, but NEXT GENERATION experience as well, to work these scripts up. One script is presently being crafted by Maurice Hurley (presently a producer for KUNG FU: THE LEGEND CONTINUES), who served as an executive producer and writer for THE NEXT GENERATION during its first two seasons. The other script is in the capable hands of Brannon Braga and Ronald D. Moore. No details are available regarding either script, but it seems that both will somehow involve a crossover— perhaps brief and obligatory— with

members of the classic STAR TREK crew.

The Braga/Moore script is rumored to involve some sort of time-travel crossover with the old crew, while Hurley's script will only involve James T. Kirk, the one remaining member of STAR TREK's Big Three never to feature in any NEXT GENERATION story line. Oddly enough, this was not in Hurley's mind until a friend of his— an actor named William Shatner— proposed a way it could be done. (C'mon, Shatner— get a life! Let go, already!)

Hurley's story will, apparently, involve an appearance by Kirk in Picard's time. Perhaps Picard will visit a senile Kirk in an old captains' home somewhere. . . . As it stands now, the script prominently featuring Kirk has been dropped because it made Kirk a more important character than any of the NEXT GENERATION characters, a fact which did not go over very well with many of the TNG performers.

One person not involved in these scripts is Michael Piller, who has already expressed a strong interest in moving away from the STAR TREK universe in the future. He passed on a chance to be involved in the movie version because he saw the script selection process as a competition between the writers, set up by the studio, and took offense at this procedure. While only one of these two scripts will be used for the movie, there is always the possibility that, if the movie is successful enough to warrant the hoped-for sequel or sequels, the second script will wind up being made anyway. Piller has not ruled out coming in as a script doctor or in some other capacity later on, but he wished to have no part in what he apparently viewed as Paramount's cutthroat story development strategy.

TNG—THE MOTION PICTURE

The plan is to create a true epic, a real big-time movie which will stand apart from the series. The TV show's production schedule will be ending a month early, in March 1994, and movie production will begin in April 1994. If the Braga/Moore script is chosen, the only obstacle to old cast involvement will be paying the right price for the services of Leonard Nimoy and William Shatner. Both, apparently, are ready and willing. Shatner has obviously backed off from his long-time dismissal of THE NEXT GENERATION, hoping to keep his hand in for at least one more feature.

As far as production is concerned, Berman intends to utilize a combination of talent from the television series. Director, editor, composer and crew will probably be entirely motion picture based. Some actors, like Marina Sirtis, have expressed concern that some characters will be marginalized in the features, as Nichelle Nichols and George Takei were in the STAR TREK features. It's just not possible to give everyone equal screen time in a biannual movie series.

On the other hand, imagine a double episode with an extra thirty or forty million dollars tacked on to the usual production cost, and there's no doubt that the first STAR TREK—THE NEXT GENERATION film will be an impressive piece of work in every aspect. And without the decade long lag that separated the demise of the STAR TREK series from its movie reincarnation, THE NEXT GENERATION cast could easily have a much longer screen life than the previous crew, especially with more projects like DEEP SPACE NINE following close behind. In his novel FLOW MY TEARS, THE POLICEMAN SAID, Philip K. Dick threw away a brief idea referring to movies called "captainkirks," perhaps predicting, without realizing it, the longevity of Paramount's TREK franchise, which will, with different captains of course, undoubtedly run well into the next century. With any luck, this will be true for a long time to come.

MEANWHILE, BACK ON THE TUBE...

As usual, Paramount isn't about to put all its eggs in one basket— or even a mere two or three. Already, there is talk of yet another STAR TREK spin-off— or, perhaps, a continued NEXT GENERATION with a completely different crew, or may even part of the regular crew. DEEP SPACE NINE has proven that two TREK shows on the air at the same time do not undercut each other, but in fact complement each other. While details involving such a project are strictly hush-hush at this point, it seems that Rick Berman is keen on keeping his hand in on this project, too. He's obviously going to be a busy man in the years to come!

As for the concept of the series, there is a strong possibility that Will Riker could take over the command of some other ship. Jonathan Frakes has expressed a willingness to stay on the small screen as long as steady work was available. Marina Sirtis, who doesn't want her Troi character to become the marginalized Uhura of the NEXT GENERATION movies, has

also echoed a similar sentiment. But this is only one of numerous concepts kicking around. Wesley Crusher is waiting in wings, for something or other; no one knows exactly what, just yet. And Ron Moore has expressed an interest in doing a show that examines the TREK universe during the period before the adventures of James T. Kirk; or, better, yet, an all-Klingon show (this gets my vote).

Obviously, all these notions are vague, unformed and ill-defined at this point. Perhaps they are all pipe dreams and one of them, or something completely different, will eventually grace our television screens. Paramount will never overlook an opportunity to extend the parameters of the Roddenberry universe so long as it turns them a profit. As long as they don't spread it to thin, and the talent is always there, there will be a market for STAR TREK in all its myriad forms.